Practical Gardeners' Guides

THE HERB GARDEN

Philippa Back

CONTENTS

NOTES
For convenience, ease-of-growing symbols have been incorporated in the A-Z sections.
They can be interpreted as follows:
  * Easy to grow plants
 ** Plants which require more than average care
*** Temperamental or difficult to grow plants

This edition published in 1989
by Octopus Books Limited,
a division of the Octopus Publishing Group,
Michelin House,
81 Fulham Road,
London SW3 6RB

Copyright © Cathay Books, 1984

ISBN 0 7064 2590 1

Produced by Mandarin Offset
Printed and bound in Hong Kong

INTRODUCTION

The owner of a herb garden can derive great satisfaction and pleasure from the special spot that he or she has set aside to grow colourful and fragrant plants which are both pleasing to the eye and useful in the home. Herb plants can be grown among flowers and shrubs in the border or in pots and containers when space is limited, but where possible, they are best cultivated in a patch on their own.

Herb plants have been used since ancient times for the health and well-being of man. For centuries they were an essential part of everyday life, not only providing both food and medicines, but also filling other functions. For example, while chemicals are now added to water to make it fit to drink, so years ago drinking water was sweetened and purified by adding the strongly aromatic plant pennyroyal, one of the dwarf-growing mints.

When food was scarce and had to be kept over a long period of time, strong herbs with antiseptic qualities such as rosemary, thyme and mugwort were used as preservatives. These herbs used on meat not only helped to preserve it but made the meat more digestible and disguised what must otherwise have often been an unpleasant flavour.

'Herb' was the name originally used to describe any soft-stemmed plant which was of use to man. Hyssop, rosemary, bay and similar shrubs and trees were therefore not regarded as herbs. Today, however, a herb means a fragrant plant which has a medicinal or culinary value in its leaves, stems, flowers, seeds or roots.

There is no doubt that herbs are some of the easiest plants to grow, which once established need remarkably little attention. Careful thought must be given to choosing your herbs before planning the herb garden because of the size of the plants and the amount of space each herb will require. Where you have little or no choice of site, select your herbs with even greater care, choosing plants which will thrive in that particular spot.

The growing chart on pages 68-77 may help to make your choice of herbs easier and may also assist you in planning the herb garden.

CHOOSING THE HERBS

The variety of herbs is so great that your first step towards a herb garden must be to choose the plants you want to grow by identifying the purposes for which you want to grow them.

It is usual to begin with a small bed of herbs useful for cooking. A larger bed could also contain other fragrant herbs to use in herb teas, for cosmetics and pot-pourris. The choice could include herbs to use as remedies for minor ailments or simply as ornamental plants.

Bear in mind when choosing the plants that many herbs overlap in their uses. Lemon balm, for example, is used for salads, stuffings and when cooking chicken. It also provides a soothing tea to help the digestion and the fresh leaves can be used to alleviate stings and bites. Its dried leaves can be added to pot-pourris and an infusion of the herb can be used as a lotion to soothe skin irritations or added to the bath water. This versatile herb is one of many; you will discover how adaptable herbs can be.

An important point to consider when choosing your herbs is the height to which they will eventually grow and the amount of room each herb will need when fully grown. If you intend to use fresh herbs throughout the season and perhaps harvest them for drying or freezing, it will be a long time before the plants reach their maximum height and width. Until that time, interplant with annual or biennial herbs.

HERBS FOR DIFFERENT USES

When making a choice of herbs it is useful to look upon them as falling into four specific groups. These are: herbs to use in the kitchen; herbs for teas and remedies; cosmetic and fragrant herbs for pot-pourris; and some herbs for an ornamental garden. The following suggestions provide a guide to help you to make a choice for your particular needs and your particular herb garden. For detailed information on the herbs consult the A-Z of herbs.

Herbs for cooking

The following list covers herbs for a compact kitchen bed. To supply the needs of a small family throughout the year these 12 would be sufficient.

Basil is a half-hardy annual and grows about 30 cm (1 ft) high. Whether you grow sweet basil or the smaller leaved bush basil, you will need two or three plants. These will enable you to freeze or dry some leaves for winter use as well as to pick them fresh throughout the summer months. Basil is particularly good with tomatoes, either raw in salads or sprinkled over cooked tomatoes.

Bay is a small evergreen tree which, after many years, grows quite tall. This handsome plant enhances any garden and is very useful among the kitchen herbs. One plant, once established, will give you sufficient leaves for cooking as many recipes call for only part of a leaf. Bay leaves are traditionally used for flavouring fish and meat dishes, and are delicious in a rice pudding.

Chives are a must in the kitchen herb bed. A perennial plant which dies down in winter, nevertheless it can be picked over a period of many months – from early in spring to late autumn. One clump of chives would provide plenty of leaves for cooking. Their slender lance-shaped leaves add a delicate onion flavour to green salads and many cooked dishes.

Dill is another annual for the cook to use. The small finely cut feathery leaves grow profusely on a single stem. Dill grows quickly and is soon ready for picking. Two plants would be sufficient in the herb bed if the leaves only are going to be used. To grow dill for seed you would need four to five plants. Dill combines well with cucumber in salad, sauce or soup and adds flavour to fish dishes.

Marjoram is a very useful herb to grow whether it is the annual variety or one of the perennials. The new perennial marjoram which combines the flavour of the annual sweet knotted marjoram with the growing habit of the perennial English wild marjoram is the best plant to grow in a small garden. The herb bears leaves throughout the year but they have little flavour until early spring. One plant is suggested for the kitchen bed. The small oval leaves provide a good flavour in salads and meat casseroles.

Mint is a good standby in the herb bed. This well-known creeping perennial is useful in

many ways. There are several mints to choose from, but spearmint and Bowles mint have the best flavour for cooking. One plant would be enough in a small herb bed for it quickly spreads in a season and would soon provide sufficient leaves for using fresh and for freezing or drying. The familiar flavour of mint adds liveliness to all salads and many sweet and savoury dishes.

Parsley is sometimes thought of as a rather ordinary herb, unimportant in the scheme of things. But it is an indispensably versatile plant and should be included in every kitchen herb bed. Though usually grown as a biennial, the plants will sometimes grow on for two to three years. Two plants are sufficient, producing lots of leaves for freezing, drying or using freshly picked.

Rosemary is a perennial shrub and a lovely herb to grow in any garden. One plant placed in an undisturbed spot in the herb bed will provide more than enough leaves for cooking. Since the flavour is strong, few leaves are required to add a distinctive flavour to meat dishes and salads based on pulses.

Sage is another perennial shrub, but it takes up less space in the herb bed than rosemary. That the fresh leaves can be picked throughout the year is a great help to the cook. One plant will suffice. Sage can be added to soups, sauces and meat dishes, as well as to stuffing.

Savory Summer savory is an annual plant; the neat attractive winter savory is a perennial. Two or three summer savory plants would be needed in the kitchen herb bed to give you enough leaves for picking, freezing or drying. One winter savory plant would be sufficient, as it is a larger plant and has many more leaves, which – despite the name – can be picked throughout the year. While summer savory has a more delicate flavour, both savories are good for seasoning bean dishes.

Tarragon is a perennial herb but dies down in winter. It is delicious for picking fresh through the summer months. One plant will provide plenty of leaves, but make sure you purchase a French tarragon plant as it has a far better flavour than the Russian tarragon. Use the leaves with savoury foods, sauces and salads.

Thyme is a small evergreen herb with leaves that can be picked all year round. One plant of garden thyme would suffice as it grows quickly. There are many varieties of thyme from which to choose, but those used in cooking are garden thyme, lemon thyme and wild thyme. The tiny leaves can be added to meat and fish dishes as well as to other savoury foods.

Herbs for teas and home remedies

A garden of 12 plants for teas and remedies can give a profusion of colour and fragrance.

Bergamot is a perennial herb with red, pink or mauve flowers according to variety. Two plants in a small garden will produce plenty of leaves to make a refreshing tea which is also soothing for sore throats. The flowers of the red variety can be eaten in salads.

Borage is a blue-flowered annual which grows rather untidily but is very pretty to look at. One plant will produce enough young leaves to make cooling summer drinks either on their own or added to wine cups and non-alcoholic drinks. Borage tea is a tonic and slightly laxative. Use the flowers to decorate the drinks or add them to green salads.

Chamomile is a feathery annual with a lovely scent and a great number of little white flowers.

Make sure it is the German chamomile when you buy the seed or a plant. To provide a good quantity of flowers grow as many plants as you can in the available space. Use the flower heads only to make a delicious tonic tea, good for the digestion and for sound sleep.

Fennel is a tall, elegant perennial herb with feathery leaves, similar in appearance to dill but with a stronger aniseed-like flavour. There are several varieties to choose from including an annual dwarf fennel, the base of which is eaten as a vegetable. Fennel grows quite quickly and one plant will provide ample leaves for picking as well as for freezing or drying. Use the leaves to make a pleasant tasting tea to settle the digestion. A strong solution of fennel makes an effective lotion for soothing tired eyes.

Lady's Mantle is an attractive perennial plant which, in mild areas, stays green throughout the winter. It is a low-growing herb and, until established in the garden, two or three plants would be needed to give sufficient leaves for picking. Lady's mantle is a medicinal and cosmetic herb. Juice from the leaves applied to the skin will help to cure acne.

Lemon Balm is a lemon-scented perennial. If the old stems are cut down in autumn, the plant will throw up new shoots providing leaves throughout the winter. One plant would be sufficient for picking, freezing or drying. Use the leaves to make a refreshing tea, soothing and calming, which can be drunk either hot or cold. Add fresh leaves to iced apple juice for a cool summer drink. Hot tea aids perspiration in feverish colds and is good for indigestion. Use crushed leaves in a poultice as a remedy for spots, boils and insect bites.

Marshmallow, once established, is a tall hardy perennial with pale rose flowers. The plant dies right down in winter. It has a place in the herb garden for its use as a remedy for minor ailments. Several plants would be needed for it is the root, when dried, which is used to make a cold soothing tea to be taken for diarrhoea and vomiting. A poultice made from the grated root helps to reduce inflammations.

Parsley is a herb mainly used in cooking but the leaves, especially those of the plain leaved variety, make a pleasant tea which is mildly laxative and an excellent remedy for haemorrhoids. It is well worth having one or two parsley plants of both the plain and curly leaved varieties to meet all the various requirements in the home.

Peppermint is a hardy creeping perennial with highly aromatic leaves. The leaves are a handsome blackish green colour and the pale mauve flowers are attractive. One plant will soon spread to provide sufficient leaves for picking to use fresh or for freezing or drying. The leaves make a fragrant tea, delicious hot or iced, which is good for the digestion and hiccups. Crushed peppermint leaves rubbed over the forehead and temples are cooling in hot weather and will cure an incipient headache.

Rosemary has so many uses that it is essential in any herb garden. It is an evergreen herb and one plant would give you enough leaves for most purposes. Rosemary tea is a pleasant drink to take as a remedy for headaches, colds and nervous depression.

Thyme is another evergreen perennial herb which makes an attractive plant in the garden and has countless uses. One plant of garden thyme would provide leaves for teas and remedies. Apart from its importance in the kitchen, an infusion of the leaves can be used as a gargle for a sore throat. Thyme tea is sedative and good for coughs. Inhalation of a hot infusion of thyme will help to ease bronchitis.

Verbascum is a tall perennial with a single stem growing out of a flat rosette of leaves. The flowers are a brilliant yellow. One or more plants would be needed to give enough flowers. It is the flowers only that are used to make a soothing tea which is taken for bronchitis and persistent coughs. This colourful tea, which must be carefully strained through muslin before drinking, is a most effective remedy.

Herbs for cosmetics and pot-pourris

Not many plants are needed to provide you with a sufficient quantity of each herb to make a wide variety of your own natural beauty preparations. The cosmetic herbs combine with herbs for pot-pourri – those fragrant plants, which when dried, hold their colour and scent to give sweet-smelling mixtures throughout the year. A list of 12 herbs is given here.

Caraway is a biennial plant which, in the second year, quickly goes to seed, and this is all to the good because it is the seeds only which are used in pot-pourris. Several plants will be necessary to provide enough. The seeds are dried then crushed or pounded before being added to the pot-pourri mixture. Caraway helps other dried herbs in the mixture to retain their scent.

Chamomile plants will be required in quantity to ensure a sufficient number of flowers to make cosmetic preparations. The dried flowers can also be added to pot-pourri mixtures. An infusion of chamomile is effective as a rinse for blonde hair, and can be used daily as a refreshing skin cleanser especially for oily skins. Use chamomile once a week in a facial steam as a deep cleanser. A hand cream made with chamomile has a softening quality, while its mild scent will stay on the skin for hours.

Fennel is an important plant to have in the cosmetic herb garden. One plant of this tall perennial will produce enough leaves and seeds for both cooking and cosmetic preparations. An infusion made with the leaves is a refreshing skin tonic and can be used on all types of skin. Fennel tea taken once a day is a natural aid in a slimming programme. A face pack of the leaves helps to smooth wrinkles and soften the complexion. Crushed fennel seed can be used as a substitute for the leaves during winter.

Lavender is a familiar shrubby perennial and an essential plant in any herb garden. Its long-lasting scent makes lavender an important ingredient in pot-pourri mixtures or even to have in bowls on its own. Two plants once established would provide enough flowers for drying. There are several varieties of lavender but the English lavender has the strongest scent. An infusion of lavender makes a sweet-smelling hair rinse and a strong decoction of the fresh flowers gives a delicious fragrance to bath water.

Lemon Balm, included among the herbs for teas and remedies, is another herb for the cosmetic garden. One plant will produce more than enough leaves for use. A strong decoction of fresh leaves, either with other herbs or on its own, adds a lovely fragrance to the bath water. A herb vinegar, made with plenty of lemon balm leaves, patted on to the skin is a refreshing way to ease a headache. An infusion of lemon balm soothes and softens irritations of the skin and smooths wrinkles.

Lemon Verbena is a handsome perennial shrub with fragrant leaves and flowers. One or two plants would suffice for, once established, they grow quite large. An infusion of the sweet-smelling leaves is a good skin lotion which can also be used for cleaning the teeth. Dried lemon verbena is lovely in pot-pourri mixtures.

Marigold Pot marigold is a colourful annual which flowers throughout the summer months. Marigold petals can be used in beauty preparations and pot-pourri mixtures. Five or six plants would be needed to give you enough

flowers for picking. Use an infusion of the petals to make a refreshing antiseptic lotion which is useful as a skin toner. Marigold petal ointment makes an efficient remedy for all skin blemishes, and soothes sunburn.

Mint is a fragrant herb to grow in the cosmetic garden and for pot-pourri mixtures. There are numerous different varieties to choose from of which the two most useful in this garden are peppermint and eau-de-Cologne mint. Two or three plants of each would suffice. Both mints can be used in a herbal bath and both, dried and crushed, give a lovely perfume to pot-pourris. Peppermint can be used to make toilet water and an infusion of peppermint leaves makes a soothing and refreshing foot bath for tired feet.

Orris is a perennial iris with handsome large white flowers. Several plants would be required and these must be allowed to mature before you use the rhizome, cleaned, dried and powdered, to add to pot-pourri mixtures. As the rhizome dries, it develops a strong scent of violets.

Rose Geranium is an unusual perennial plant normally grown in pots or containers. It can be transferred to the herb garden in the summer. Rose geranium provides strong rose-scented leaves which add a lovely perfume to pot-pourri mixtures.

Rosemary should not be omitted from any herb garden, because of its perennial shrubby growth and its leaves that can be used all the year round. It has a place in the cosmetic garden for its leaves make hair lotions and shampoos for dark hair, herbal baths and soothing baths for weary feet. An infusion of rosemary helps to lighten freckles and is used as a skin tonic. Dried leaves give a lasting perfume to pot-pourri mixtures.

Salad Burnet is a neat growing perennial of which is it worth having one or two plants. The leaves have astringent properties; when made into a lotion they help to refine the skin and close the pores. The lotion also cleanses the skin and is refreshing and beneficial to use on a hot summer's day.

Ornamental herbs

Because a collection of old fashioned herbs is decorative, it does not imply that you cannot use the plants. Lavender and rosemary are two herbs which have always been valued in gardens for their beauty. The six herbs suggested for this garden were all grown in the past for their medicinal properties, though modern methods of treatment have now overtaken them.

Camphor makes a showy plant in the decorative herb garden with a mass of tiny, white daisy-like flowers with brilliant yellow centres. The whole plant smells of camphor which is not unpleasant and it is useful for flower arrangements.

Hyssop is an attractive perennial well worth growing in the ornamental garden. The blue, pink or white flowers have a lovely scent which attracts bees and they have a long flowering period. A plant of each colour in the bed makes a colourful trio.

Jacob's Ladder is a neat growing perennial and highly decorative in the garden. There are two varieties, one with white and one with blue flowers. One or two plants take up little space in the herb bed. Originally the leaves were used for healing cuts.

Sage has several varieties which are most attractive and all are perennials. One plant each of pineapple sage and purple sage are suggested for the ornamental garden. The leaves of the former are sweetly fragrant and those of purple sage are a handsome colour.

Soapwort is a creeping perennial ornamental herb. One plant will soon increase sufficiently to give a mass of pale pink flowers in June. The flowers have little scent but are very showy. An infusion of soapwort was, and still is today, used for washing delicate fabrics.

Thyme amply justifies a place in the ornamental garden. Garden thyme produces highly decorative flowers and there are other variegated thymes which have colourful foliage continuing throughout the year. Five or six plants set together make a solid patch which is very fragrant and attracts bees.

RIGHT: The different greens of the herbs are attractive in this carefully planned bed

PLANNING AND PREPARATION

You will have success from the start if you remember a number of important points when choosing a site for your herb garden.

PLANNING THE SITE

First, the aspect must be carefully considered, as most herbs require some sunshine during the day. Many herbs originate from the warmer climate of those countries bordering the Mediterranean so the perfect position will be achieved if the herb bed can face south and west. Where the only possible place for your herbs is in partial shade, choose varieties that thrive in such a situation. Chervil, sweet cicely, bergamot, woodruff, angelica, chives and any one of the mints grow well in semi-shaded areas. A shady herb bed should have adequate protection from the north easterly winds. Ideally this protection should be in the form of a fence or wall rather than a hedge which, unless it is a useful herb, will be competing with the herbs for food, light and water. A hedge also harbours pests and diseases.

Herbs which are in frequent use need to be in a bed as near as possible to the house, so that they are convenient to reach when the weather is very wet.

The herb bed should consist of good garden soil (see also page 19) to encourage steady growth during the harvest season.

Size is another important consideration. When planning the herb garden allow 30-45 cm (12-18 inches) between the larger plants. Rosemary and sage, for example, need plenty of space when they are fully grown and it is better not to move them once they are established. While they are small you can plant annual or biennial herbs among them. Herbs of medium height need 30 cm (12 inches) between the plants; for small herbs 15-20 cm (6-8 inches) will be sufficient. Mint is a herb which can spread quickly in one season and may need to be contained.

Finally, you must be able to reach the herbs easily whatever the size of the bed. Plant to leave space for paths or stepping stones so that you can pick the herbs without treading on other plants or getting wet and muddy feet.

HERB GARDEN DESIGNS

Traditionally herbs were set out in a formal pattern, often of complicated design. Nowadays a simple arrangement of plants is easier to maintain and, if kept neat and tidy, can be a pleasure to look at as well as to use. To set the herbs too closely in a bed and allow them to grow unchecked would soon bring disappointment especially if you wished to use the herbs to any extent. Since the plants would all be

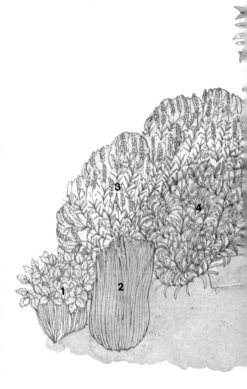

struggling upwards for light the lanky weak-looking herbs would have little flavour or scent.

The following suggestions for herb garden designs can easily be adapted to your own use.

In a large garden a semi-formal herb bed looks particularly effective. Curves, squares and rectangles can be combined in a definite pattern, criss-crossed with paths for easy access to the herbs.

The rather large country garden plan shows how a more formal design can be set out, which herbs to grow and where to place them. The taller perennials are set at the back of the bed where they can grow undisturbed. A low re-taining wall or a fence on the north side will help to protect the herbs from cold winds. One or two stepping stones placed at strategic points will make it easier for picking and tending the herbs.

1 SALAD BURNET, 2 WELSH ONION, 3 LAVENDER, 4 FRENCH TARRAGON, 5 LEMON THYME, 6 LEMON BALM, 7 BAY, 8 SAGE, 9 CARAWAY THYME, 10 ROSEMARY, 11 PENNYROYAL, 12 SWEET CICELY, 13 LOVAGE, 14 BORAGE, 15 CHERVIL, 16 PARSLEY, 17 APPLE MINT, 18 HYSSOP, 19 ENGLISH WILD MARJORAM, 20 MARIGOLD

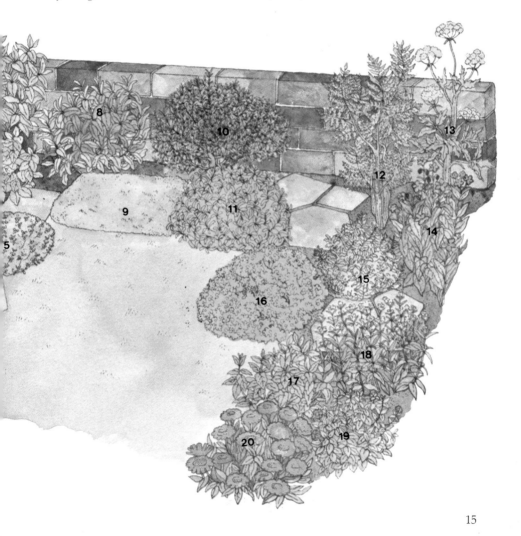

The semi-circular herb bed lends itself well to the smaller town garden where it may be difficult to find a really sunny position for it. Bay could be replaced with lovage if the bed gets little sun. Chervil is a hardy bi-annual and could be replaced by bergamot making it an all-perennial bed of herbs. In place of tarragon, which prefers a sunny position, you could grow salad burnet. Flat stones are placed so you can easily reach all the herbs.

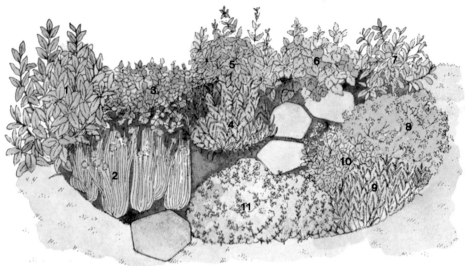

1 BAY, 2 CHIVES, 3 CHERVIL, 4 FRENCH TARRAGON, 5 MINT, 6 LEMON BALM, 7 SAGE, 8 PARSLEY, 9 WINTER SAVORY, 10 MARJORAM, 11 THYME

An easy herb bed in a cottage garden uses one wall of the house as the protected side of the bed and perhaps sites the bed adjacent to the kitchen door. A low hedge of lavender could be planted round one side to give further protection. Marigold and dill are the only annuals in this bed which could be replaced by others the following season.

1 SAGE, 2 MARJORAM, 3 FRENCH TARRAGON, 4 ROSEMARY, 5 DILL, 6 PARSLEY, 7 THYME, 8 WINTER SAVORY, 9 CHIVES, 10 MARIGOLD, 11 LAVENDER

Where space is very limited, a raised herb bed is a good idea. The plants get more light and you can provide them with a greater depth of soil. This will enable you to grow some of the taller herbs very successfully as well as the low growing ones.

Raise the bed to a depth of 60 cm (2 ft) with a south-facing wall. There is a wide choice of herbs for this type of bed. Nasturtium, an annual, will clamber all over the back wall and look very colourful. The raised bed full of aromatic herbs can be a pleasure to the disabled; those who are blind can enjoy the fragrance of the herbs.

1 ROSE GERANIUM, 2 MARJORAM, 3 BASIL, 4 THYME, 5 CHIVES, 6 HYSSOP, 7 CALAMINT, 8 NASTURTIUM

A very simple herb bed and one easy to maintain year after year can be made by using old roofing slates. These can be obtained from demolition yards. Set the slates on edge to form rectangles side by side. Placed along the side of a path the herbs are easy to reach. Fill the sections with small clumps of herbs such as chives, parsley, garden thyme and mint. Plant a few annuals also; try summer savory, sweet marjoram, marigold and dill.

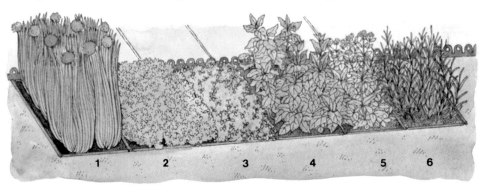

1 CHIVES, 2 PARSLEY, 3 THYME, 4 MINT, 5 SWEET MARJORAM, 6 WINTER SAVORY

Herbs can be grown successfully on a sloping south-facing bank so long as the bank is not too steep or the soil so light that it will be washed away by a shower of rain. Where the soil is mostly clay it will retain moisture and be perfectly suitable for herbs; otherwise it is best to terrace the bed by building a low retaining wall. The herbs suggested for this bed are all perennials. Note that the mints are in the lowest part of the bank where they will get most moisture. If the bank is large and needs stepping stones make sure they are absolutely level.

There are, of course, many more ways in which you can set out your own herb garden bearing in mind the points set out above.

1 CHIVES, 2 FRENCH TARRAGON, 3 BERGAMOT, 4 FENNEL, 5 LEMON BALM, 6 SAGE, 7 LOVAGE, 8 ROSEMARY, 9 HYSSOP, 10 ORRIS, 11 EAU DE COLOGNE MINT, 12 SWEET CICELY, 13 SPEARMINT

Paths and edges

The importance of paths in providing essential access to every part of the herb garden cannot be overemphasized. Construct the paths of brick or paving slabs laid on to sand, or use concrete. All can look attractive as well as being functional. Do not lay grass paths as they are difficult to keep neat and trim.

A herb bed is easier to maintain if it has properly constructed edges, which can be of brick, concrete slabs or timber. An edging between lawn and herb bed will allow you to clip the lawn edge without the grass cuttings going over the herbs. A permanent edging also allows small creeping plants like pennyroyal and thyme to spill over the edge of the slabs.

A herb bed lends itself particularly well to being enclosed. A surrounding wall, fence or hedge, serves as a windbreak and reduces the danger of exposed plants being killed in winter. A wall is a permanent surround and can look attractive – one or more courses of brick or kerbstone create a neat edging. A low fence about 30 cm (12 inches) high constructed of wattle or strips of wood is less permanent but gives a softer outline. The traditional surround for a herb garden was the boxwood hedge but this takes goodness and moisture from the soil, to the detriment of the herbs. The most useful surround is a low hedge of lavender, germander, hyssop, thyme or sage. Lavender, sage and hyssop would need to be well trimmed.

PREPARATION OF THE HERB BED

Once you have decided on the site and chosen the herbs you wish to grow in your herb garden it is important to take trouble over the preparation of the bed. You should first peg out the dimensions and lay out paths and edges.

Preparing the soil

Soil which is a good medium for growing plants should be a balanced mixture of lime, sand, humus and clay. There should also be good drainage for easy working. This type of soil is easier to dig or fork over, and it warms up early in the spring giving a longer growing period. Soil conditions such as these are rarely found in the garden but with a little concentrated work applying compost, manure or rotted leaves, your soil will produce the right medium.

Drainage is most important where the soil is heavily compacted or consists largely of clay. If this is your problem, a drainage trench set in the lowest point in the garden must be provided. Dig a hole 60 cm (2 ft) wide by 60 cm (2 ft) deep and fill it to 45 cm (18 inches) with rubble or large stones, then replace the top soil.

Digging is important in the preparation of the herb bed. A heavy soil should be dug during the autumn to allow winter frosts to break it down. A sandy light soil can be dug during the winter or early spring but not in frosty weather.

A few weeks after digging is completed, sprinkle hydrated lime over the soil and leave it for the rain to wash in. Herbs require a well-limed soil, though if too much is added the leaves will turn yellow. A chalky soil will not need liming, but for all other soils lime is a good conditioner. It helps to bind together very sandy soil and breaks down heavy clay soil making it easier to work. Hydrated lime improves the soil and helps to keep the herbs free of pests, acting as a valuable natural insecticide. Lime neutralizes sour or acid soil, encouraging earthworms and useful bacteria to flourish which otherwise are absent in this type of soil. Lime is widely available from garden shops.

Once the herb bed is prepared, place any stepping stones required into position. Set flat stones on to well packed sand, making sure the stones are level and firm enough to stand on. Leave the herb bed to settle for two or three weeks before planting the herbs.

BELOW LEFT: Making a drainage hole
BELOW: Pegging out the herb bed

Preventing weeds

The simplest method of producing a weed-free herb bed is to lay suitable black polythene film over the soil with holes cut out for the plants. The sheeting can be bought from garden shops and centres and comes in varying widths. It offers several advantages: the polythene will last in the same place for two or three years, which helps the new herbs to become established without disturbance; it prevents any loss of water by evaporation; in a hot dry season it forms condensation which keeps the soil moist beneath the plastic, and it acts like a 'mulch' for the herbs, so that only occasionally do the herbs need watering. The black polythene smothers weeds by shutting out the light, allowing all the goodness in the soil to be available to the herbs.

Prepare the herb bed as described on page 19 and leave the earth to settle for two or three weeks before putting down the polythene. Cut sufficient film to cover the herb bed and stretch it down over the soil. The neatest way to anchor the outer edge is to bury it under a surround of narrow paving slabs. An alternative is to dig a trench to a depth of 5-7 cm (2-3 inches) along the edge of the bed and bury about 10 cm (4 inches) of the film. Fill in the trench with soil or pebbles. This is best done on a calm day as the plastic is light and easily caught by the wind.

When ready to start planting, first lay out the various herbs on top of the polythene in the position you have already planned for them. According to the type of herb, take a flower pot of appropriate diameter, stand it on the plastic and with a sharp knife cut a neat circle around the pot. Remove the disc and, using a trowel, plant the herb. For dwarf herbs and seedlings make a hole 6 cm (2½ inches) in diameter. For larger, container-grown herbs make a hole 10 cm (4 inches) in diameter. When the herbs are in place, hide the shiny black plastic by covering it with peat, gravel or sterilized soil.

HERBS IN CONTAINERS

You can successfully use containers both large and small to grow herbs. Wooden troughs, urns of stone or plastic, old sinks and large flower pots are all suitable. The containers can be put on a patio or terrace, or a narrow box full of herbs can be set against a wall. A collection of herbs can be grown in a hanging basket.

Herbs can be grown indoors in pots and containers. They need more care and attention as herbs naturally require a great deal of light to help them make good growth and produce flavour and scent. Herbs grown indoors also need more feeding and watering.

BELOW: Using black polythene to control weeds
RIGHT: A variety of herbs grown in containers

PLANTING AND ROUTINE CARE

Once you have chosen the herbs and prepared the bed, it is time to buy plants and seeds.

PURCHASING THE HERBS

Nowadays most garden centres sell a good selection of container-grown herbs, but there are nurseries specializing in herbs where you will find a wider variety of both the common herbs and their variegated species as well as the more unusual ones. At a herb nursery you will be able to see fully grown plants which will give you some idea of how your own herb garden will look when the plants are established.

Take with you to the herb nursery or garden centre a list of the herbs you want together with their Latin names. It is easy to get confused over the common names of herbs and it is important to purchase the correct ones.

When selecting herbs there are one or two points to remember. First, look for the fibrous root formation coming out of the base of the pot. This signifies that it is a well established plant which will have a greater chance of surviving. Second, choose sturdy plants in preference to tall ones with masses of growth, because the large herbs may have been too long in the pot and will take longer to establish themselves.

PLANTING HERB PLANTS

Give container-grown plants a good watering when you get them home, then leave them overnight. When planting remove the herbs carefully from the containers so as to disturb the root ball as little as possible. Plant out the herbs setting them in so that the soil comes just over the root ball. Woody stemmed herbs should be planted to the depth of the 'soil mark' on the stems. It is important not to crowd the roots, so make the planting hole sufficiently deep and wide to provide space for the roots which should be carefully spread out. Put a handful of compost in the bottom of the hole to give the herbs a good start and cover it thinly with soil. Once all the herbs are planted give them another good watering.

RAISING HERBS FROM SEED

At a herb nursery you will be able to find both

ABOVE AND LEFT: Planting container-grown herbs
ABOVE RIGHT: Planting woody stemmed herbs

annual and perennial container-grown herbs to give you a ready-made herb garden. This method is quick and easy but it can be costly. Many herbs can be grown cheaply and successfully from seed.

The annual herbs are easy to grow from seed and give you two added advantages. First, if you can sow the seed really early you will have plants that will be as good as, or better than, the container-grown herbs on sale in late spring. Second, you will be able to start picking and using the herbs earlier in the season. As early as February you can start sowing herbs indoors.

Herbs should be raised in well-scrubbed boxes. Add a small quantity of household disinfectant to the scrubbing water to reduce the risk of mildew and other diseases. Fill the boxes

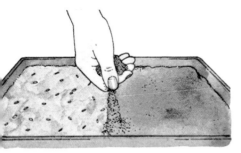

Sow seed sparingly (above) and cover seed boxes with glass and newspaper (below)

Remove covering once seedlings have germinated (above) and pot the herbs on when each has four leaves (below)

temperature is more or less constant and not above 15°C (60°F). Once germination has occurred, remove glass and newspaper and leave the seedlings to grow until each one has four leaves. Pot the herbs on by setting them out 5 cm (2 inches) apart in boxes or in flower pots, filled with potting compost.

When the seedlings have 8-10 leaves, start hardening them off by carrying the boxes or pots outside during the day in warm weather. After a week to ten days, plant the herbs out.

Herb seed sown out of doors has to take its chance with the weather, so do not sow too early. Wait until all danger from frost is over, usually about May. Sow the seed directly into the herb bed and cover lightly with compost. Seed sown too deeply will not germinate. Once the seedlings are growing well, thin the plants to the recommended distance apart. If the weather is cloudy and cold put a cloche over the seeds to help them to germinate.

Perennial herbs can also be grown successfully from seed. Fennel, sage, lovage, hyssop and salad burnet are all easy to grow. Other herbs such as sweet cicely, parsley and some of the thymes take time to germinate. It is necessary to buy plants of the perennial French tarragon as it does not set seed. The slow-growing shrubby herbs rosemary, bay and lemon verbena are best bought as container-grown plants. An advantage in purchasing container-grown perennial herbs is that they can be planted out at any time of year provided the weather is warm and moist.

PLANTING IN CONTAINERS

To grow herbs in containers make sure the vessel is large enough to give all the requirements it needs when fully grown. Do not plant too many herbs in one pot. Different herbs can be set into a single container provided they each need the same amount of soil, light, air and watering. Set the containers, whether indoors or outside, in their permanent positions. Fill with a mixture of good soil and compost almost to the rim of the container and firm down the soil. If the container is too full of soil there will be no room for the extra soil which clings to the herb when planting. Leave space at the top of the container for watering and for adding extra plant food in later months. Water the soil well and leave for 24 hours before planting.

with a good seed compost. Water the compost and leave it for 24 hours before sowing the seed. Firm down the compost and sow the seed sparingly on top. Cover lightly with a little extra compost and firm down again. Cover the boxes with a piece of glass and then a layer of newspaper until the seed has germinated. Set the boxes in a greenhouse or warm place where the

23

ROUTINE CARE

A simple programme of routine care, if carried out regularly, will provide you with a constant supply of lovely fragrant plants.

In the herb garden it is important to keep the ground free of weeds, which compete with the herbs for food and light. Hand-weed the bed when the plants are small so as not to disturb the roots. Hoe carefully between established herbs at regular intervals. This will help not only to keep down the weeds but will loosen the soil round the herbs so they get sufficient water. To prevent loss of water through evaporation, put peat round the plants, then hoe later in the season. In a long spell of dry weather water the plants in the evenings when the sun has gone down. If your herbs are set in black polythene film there should be few weeds and very little watering will be necessary.

Organic fertilizers such as bone meal, hoof and horn and dried blood can be applied in the spring to act throughout the growing season. Compost is valuable in supplying the soil with humus. After using it in the preparation of the herb bed, compost can be forked lightly into the top soil in summer or used as a mulch to retain moisture round the plants.

In an ornamental or decorative herb garden where the plants will not be subjected to continued cutting then the addition of bone meal or compost such as is given to a herbaceous bed is all that will be required. In a herb garden where a considerable amount of the herb plant will be harvested a more than average amount of nutrients must be added to the soil to allow the plants to recover before the winter.

Be on the lookout for pests or signs of disease in the herbs and deal with them promptly to keep the plants in good condition.

Once a fortnight in the growing season water the herbs with a liquid fertilizer, available from garden centres. This is necessary because if you are constantly picking the leaves the plants need extra food to ensure continued strong growth.

As they appear, cut off the flower heads of those herbs whose leaves you wish to gather so that the full flavour and scent will be concentraded there. Cut off the flowers of chamomile and verbascum for drying as soon as they are fully opened. This is a tedious task but one worth the effort as all the value of the plant goes into the flowers and this disappears as the flower fades.

In early spring or in the autumn spread a small amount of organic plant food over the herb bed and gently fork it in. Do not give the herbs too much fertilizer or the plants will grow too quickly and have little scent or flavour as a result. Before winter sets in, take up the annuals. Cut off the dying stems at the base of those perennials which die down. Put in stakes for these plants, in case you forget where they are next year. Cut back a little of the year's growth on woody-stemmed herbs so that they will not straggle and break, but form strong bushy growth.

A number of herbs can be dug up and put into pots to keep indoors for the winter. Chives, mint, parsley and marjoram will overwinter happily inside a greenhouse, a frame or in the house. Other herbs such as pineapple sage and rose geranium will not survive the winter outside and have to be brought into warmth during the winter months.

Herbs kept indoors need a good supply of water and should never be allowed to dry out. In the winter, take care not to let the atmosphere become too dry – central heating can be a killer. A bowl of water next to the herbs will keep the air round the plants humid.

Make sure herbs in containers and those indoors are regularly supplied with plant food. With only a limited amount of soil in the containers it can soon become impoverished.

PROPAGATION

Once the herbs are established in the garden you can easily increase the number of plants yourself rather than buying in new ones. The simplest way, in late season, is to allow the flowers on one or two stems to go to seed. Leave the seeds to fall on the soil and new seedlings will soon appear. Angelica and lovage are best dealt with by this method, for their seed will only germinate when absolutely fresh. With other herbs, remove the seeds and sow them in spring in the usual manner. Treat annual herbs in this way.

There are a number of herbs which never or very rarely set seed. To increase your stock of these plants other methods have to be used. Provided you choose the right time of year to be sure of success, you can build up the number of herbs by taking stem or root cuttings, by root division or by layering shoots or branches.

Stem cuttings

These are best taken during the summer months from a well-established herb, as long as you do not take too many off one plant at any one time. Take the cutting from a new shoot and not from one which shows signs of flowering. Cut the stem 10-15 cm (4-6 inches) long just below a leaf bud and remove all leaves from the lower half of the cutting. Dip the cut end into water, shake off the drops, then dip it into rooting powder. Plant the cutting firmly into a pot filled with moist potting compost. Put the pot in the shade until you see signs of growth and keep the soil damp.

Another method is to put the cuttings into a shallow pot or seed box full of sharp sand. Rooting powder and sharp sand are available at garden shops. If you plan to take many cuttings set them in a shallow trench in the garden. Run a little sharp sand along the bottom of the

trench, set in the cuttings and firm down the soil round them.

Some of the shrubby herbs such as rosemary or lemon verbena may take weeks to start growing, so give the cuttings plenty of time before you discard them. As soon as the cuttings have rooted, which will be evident from the appearance of new fresh leaves at the top, they can be planted in their permanent positions.

Root cuttings

Take these in the autumn from herbs such as angelica and marshmallow. The mints too can be increased in this way. When lifting the plant cut pieces of the root about 1 cm (¼ inch) thick and chop them in 5 cm (2 inch) lengths. Fill a seed box half full of potting compost and lay the roots on top. Cover the roots with about 1.5 cm (½ inch) more soil. Give the seed box a good watering and set it in the shade. Cover with a piece of glass and then a sheet of newspaper until signs of growth appear. Transplant the herbs into pots for planting out later.

BELOW: Take stem cuttings from a new shoot and remove bottom leaves

BELOW: Chop root cuttings into 5 cm (2 inch) lengths and set in a seed box to germinate.

Root division

This has to be done in early spring or in the autumn when the herb has either become too large for the bed or when it is going to be moved. If it has been a good growing season some herbs put on an enormous amount of growth, so dividing the plants is an easy method of increasing your stock.

Carefully dig up the whole herb and, using a spade, cut the plant into smaller clumps, or pull the roots apart if it is easier. Replant the divided roots into their new permanent positions and give them plenty of water until they are established.

Layering

An easy way to increase herbs, this can be done at any time of the year. Creeping species such as mints layer themselves, but others like rosemary and sage need help. Choose a strong growing branch close to the ground and, about 25 cm (10 inches) from the tip of the branch, make a small slanting cut. Moisten the cut with water and put some rooting powder on to it. Make a small hole in the soil and fill it with compost or sharp sand. Gently bend the branch down and bury the cut in the hole. Firm the soil

BELOW: Pull the roots apart to divide a small plant
BOTTOM: Make sure the branch to be layered is firmly secured in the ground

over the cut and secure it with a piece of bent wire stuck into the ground. Make sure the layered piece will not blow about otherwise the branch will bob up again. After about five to six weeks the branch should have taken root. Cut the rooted stem from the main plant and set it into its new position.

HARVESTING THE HERBS

In summer, herb leaves and flowers can be freshly picked as you require them. To ensure a good supply of your favourite herbs through the winter you can freeze them or, if no freezer is available, dry the herbs and store them in glass jars in a cupboard. Herbs gathered for preserving must be at their best for fragrance and flavour; the right time for this varies from herb to herb. As a rule cut the herb just before the plant comes into flower. Do not cut the whole plant; take only the best sprigs or leaves, otherwise the herb will not survive.

There are some exceptions to these general rules for harvesting herbs. Summer savory and thyme are gathered when the plant is in full flower. Bay leaves can be picked individually all the year round. Tarragon should be picked when it has grown about 30 cm (12 inches) high. When harvesting the bushy perennials lovage and fennel, cut back to about one third of their growth each time – they soon recover and produce plenty more fresh young leaves. Woody-stemmed perennial herbs can be preserved in small quantities during the summer months by cutting a few sprigs at a time. Otherwise have a grand freezing or drying session in the autumn after cutting the plants back to half the year's growth.

During the growing season annual herbs for preserving such as basil, chervil and dill can be cut down to within 15 cm (6 inches) of the base. In the autumn when you remove the plant altogether you can take another crop of leaves to freeze or dry.

Herbs are best gathered in the morning after dew has evaporated and before the heat of the sun is too great to affect the flavour. Try not to crush the leaves as you pick them. Wash the leaves gently in water if necessary and shake off the excess. No washing is necessary for flowers, petals or seeds. Roots which are dried need a good scrub to make sure all the soil is removed.

PRESERVING HERBS

It is of course very useful to be able to preserve your herbs and this can be done by freezing and by drying.

Freezing herbs

One of the simplest ways of preserving your herbs is to freeze them; indeed there are many which are better frozen than dried. Basil, mint, parsley and tarragon all freeze very well and retain their full flavour. The leaves for freezing should be clean and dry – discard any that are not perfect. Pick the leaves from the stems and place the individual herbs in small plastic bags or in plastic wrap. Freeze tarragon in sprigs rather than picking off the leaves. It is better to have a number of bags with a little herb in each as usually only a small quantity is needed in a recipe. You can mix two or three herbs together in one bag ready to add to a stew or casserole. Place all the bags in one large plastic bag so they do not get lost in the freezer. Chopped fresh herbs can be frozen by adding them to water in ice cube trays; when you want to use one, simply melt a cube.

Drying herbs

Herbs dried properly will remain green and retain all the flavour and scent of the plant. The process of cutting, drying and storing the herbs needs to be done as quickly as possible. Obviously thick fleshy leaves, flowers, petals and seeds will take longer to dry.

There are a number of points to remember when drying your herbs. With the exception of bay, use whole stems of leafy specimens rather than stripping off the leaves. Chives and Welsh onion tops should be washed and then chopped finely before drying. Spread the washed herbs out on sheets of greaseproof paper on wire cake trays. Do not pile the herb up high, but spread it out carefully – it will dry more quickly. Put the wire trays into a cool oven, or a warm airing cupboard. Leave the oven door slightly ajar so that the moisture evaporating from the leaves can escape. Always make sure that air can circulate around the trays. Never dry the leafy herbs next to chives as the strong flavour will permeate the milder herbs.

The length of drying time varies widely. Rosemary and sage take much longer than fennel or chervil. When fully dried the leaves should be crisp and friable and the stems can be discarded. Herbs should always be dried in the dark as light can affect the fragrance and flavour.

Flowers can be dried by laying them out on nylon netting stretched over a wooden frame in the airing cupboard. Small flowers and petals can be placed between sheets of newspaper and dried in a darkened airy room. Under the bed is a good place. Petals and flowers usually take from 10 to 14 days to dry and should be crisp and crackly when fully dry.

Seeds take a long time to dry. When the seed heads on the plant look dry and brown cut them off with a long stem attached. Tie the stems together carefully and lay them on newspaper so as not to lose any seeds in the process. Gently put the bunch of seed heads into a large brown paper bag and tie the bag loosely so that it does not fall off. Hang the bunch by the stems so the seed heads are upside down in the bag. As the seeds dry they will fall into the bag. After some weeks test the seeds. If the seeds smell at all musty or will easily snap in two, the seeds are not dry. Remove the seeds from the bag, spread them between sheets of brown paper and leave in an airy room for two or three weeks.

Roots and rhizomes for drying should be scrubbed until clean and cut into 5 cm (2 inch) lengths. Spread out the pieces on nylon netting so that air can circulate round them and set them in a warm dark place to dry. Both roots and rhizomes take a long time to dry, usually about six weeks, but this can vary.

Storing the herbs When the leafy herbs are dry, immediately rub the leaves from the stems by hand, crushing them into small pieces. Petals and flowers are left whole. Seeds are also stored whole – once ground they lose flavour much more rapidly.

To store your herbs for winter, place each in a screwtop jar and keep them in the dark. Do not mix herbs together in a jar unless you are making a special mixture when the quantity of each herb is carefully worked out beforehand. If you wish to store your herbs in tins, put the herb in a cotton bag before putting it into the tin. Direct contact with metal can affect the flavour. Label each jar and add the date. Dried herbs do not last forever and begin to lose their flavour after about a year. Petals, flowers and seeds can all be stored in the same manner.

PESTS AND DISEASES

Pests and diseases do not present a great problem in the herb garden because the strong aromatic oils contained in the leaves of most herbs keep the pests at bay. None will be found near camphor, thyme, lavender or juniper. Plants like these can help to control pests on more succulent herbs. Those pests which do attack the plants are fairly easy to control.

A certain amount of protection can be provided by planting the strongest smelling herbs among those that are more susceptible. It is most important that as far as possible natural organic products should be used. Chemicals might alter the flavour and scent of the herb and drive away the bees.

LEFT TO RIGHT: Caterpillar attacking young basil leaves; a snail on a young tarragon shoot; red spider mite on basil; powdery mildew on bergamot; mint rust; damping off disease on seedlings

PESTS

Caterpillars attack young leaves of basil, tarragon, sweet knotted marjoram and summer savory. The easiest solution is to remove the caterpillars by hand in a small herb bed but, if preferred, a light spray with derris powder will get rid of them. Derris powder is a perfectly safe organic insecticide and if sprayed on the herbs in the evening will not harm them for picking next day; wash the herbs before use.

Slugs and snails can be a nuisance when the weather is warm and wet; the young shoots of tarragon and bergamot are their particular favourites. A sprinkling of lime round the plants should help, or you can use slug pellets.

Another pest which in hot dry conditions might attack herbs is the red spider mite, a minute insect which attaches itself to the underside of the leaves by means of a fine web and feeds on the sap. The leaves turn a mottled

greyish brown. Usually the spider mite only appears on succulent herbs growing under glass. The remedy is to use a liquid derris spray.

DISEASES

Very few diseases are likely to appear in the herb garden. Powdery mildew does sometimes appear on bergamot, especially the pink-flowered variety, but this can be controlled by spraying with sulphur dust or a spray made from the dried stems and leaves of horsetail (*Equisetum arvense*). To make the spray use 25 g (1 oz) of horsetail to 2.75 litres (5 pints) of water. Bring to the boil and boil for 20 minutes. Allow the mixture to cool before straining and using as a spray. Use this mixture only on fully grown plants; if the process has to be repeated on the same plant, dilute the spray for the second application.

'Damping off' disease affects seedlings only. The base of the stem goes black and the plant withers. To prevent this happening do not sow the seeds too thickly in the box, do not use unsterilized compost and do not over-water.

Other ways to combat this disease are either to use a seed dressing at the outset or to water the seed boxes before sowing with a solution of Cheshunt compound, which is available at garden shops. This last process should be repeated when the seedlings appear and again when pricking them out. There are 'seed saver' preparations on the market; follow the manufacturer's instructions for use closely. If any seedlings are affected, remove and burn them, then water the remaining ones with the Cheshunt compound. Basil is particularly prone to 'damping off' disease.

Mint rust is a fungus disease which attacks all varieties of mint. The spores attack the roots then appear on the underside of the leaves and gradually spread up the stems. The only remedy is to remove the plant and burn it, then sterilize the soil with diluted Jeyes fluid.

A herb garden full of sturdy well-cared-for plants is the safest and best way to avoid pests and diseases. Keep the weeds down and water the plants in a dry spell and you will be rewarded with a trouble-free garden.

COMMON HERBS

ANGELICA*
Angelica archangelica biennial
A large handsome plant, angelica can grow to 1.8 m (6 ft) and is a lovely herb for the back of the garden in a partially shaded position where it can act as a windbreak for the more delicate herbs. The big spreading leaves are divided into three leaflets. Clusters of small greenish white flowers appear on the tops of the stems in the second year of growth.

Angelica is usually treated as a biennial, but if the flowerheads are cut off immediately the seeds set, the plant will continue to grow for a further few years. If the flowerheads are left to seed in the second year the plant will die. Angelica must be grown from seed that is absolutely fresh and must be subjected to winter frost before germination can be guaranteed. The seed which falls from the plant in the second year will germinate early the following spring to provide a mass of seedlings growing around the old plant. You can leave them quite happily to grow where they fall or you can transplant the seedlings into pots or a small trench in the garden.

It is easiest to buy your first angelica plant growing in a container. In spring set angelica into its permanent position. Once your new plant is established you can start to use the leaves although for the full flavour and scent you should wait until the second year.

Use: Angelica has a sweet scent and a pleasant but rather strong flavour. Candied angelica is well known as a cake decoration and can easily be made at home. Cut the young hollow stems into 5 cm (2 inch) lengths and boil them in a heavy sugar syrup until transparent and tender. Strain and allow the stems to dry completely before storing in screwtop jars. The candied stems impart a delicious flavour when cooked with rhubarb or gooseberries. Add young leaves to water when poaching fish and as a flavouring when making rhubarb jam. The midribs of the larger leaves can be eaten like celery. Cut them out and blanch them, by plunging them into boiling water then immediately into cold water.

Use the seeds infused in milk when making a custard. Make a herb tea using the chopped leaves to induce perspiration in a feverish cold. Add dried angelica leaves or seeds to pot-pourri mixtures.

BASIL***
Ocimum basilicum (sweet basil)
half-hardy annual
Sweet basil and a smaller leaved variety known as bush basil are the two most commonly grown. Both basils grow about 30-60 cm (1-2 ft) tall. The sweet basil has broad dark green leaves with a strong spicy smell. The leaves of bush basil are a lighter green and though smaller are very much more profuse. The spikes of small white flowers appear early in the season.

Both basils are annuals and can be grown from your own seed year after year. A word of warning about sowing basil seed out of doors: it is difficult to grow from seed outside in temperate climates. The seed takes a long time to germinate and the seedlings will not thrive until the weather is really warm. This cuts down the length of its growing season and as a result there will be fewer leaves for picking.

In early spring sow basil seeds indoors in pots or seed boxes filled with compost. Cover them with a piece of glass and a sheet of newspaper. Once the seedlings appear, remove the glass and newspaper. Do not sow the seed too thickly in the boxes because of the danger of damping-off disease. Once they have germinated, do not overwater the seedlings. When they are large enough, plant them out about 15-20 cm (6-8 inches) apart in a sunny sheltered position. The leaves are ready for picking about six weeks after planting. Pinch out the flower heads as they appear to keep all the flavour in the leaves, allowing one plant or stem to flower and set seed for next year's plants. At the end of the season, pull up the plants and keep the seed dry in a brown paper bag.

Use: The strong peppery flavour of basil makes it an ideal seasoning herb in the kitchen; it is equally good fresh and dried. Add it to all tomato dishes to bring out their full flavour. Use with soups,

salads and sauces and for spaghetti dishes.

Use a small amount of the chopped fresh leaves in vegetable salads and tomato juice. Add basil to minced beef re-cipes and to sausagemeat for sausage rolls. A few finely chopped leaves can be added to egg dishes; they add a good flavour to omelettes. Add a tiny amount to butter sauces to

Angelica is a strikingly handsome plant with attractive flowers

accompany fish and sprinkle over cooked peas and boiled potatoes.

BAY***

Laurus nobilis evergreen tree

A slow-growing small evergreen tree, bay is a handsome formal herb to have in the garden. It can grow to 12 m (40 ft) but takes many years to reach that height. The glossy dark green leaves have a leathery texture and when fully grown are about 5-7.5 cm (2-3 inches) long. Small yellow flowers bloom in early summer and are followed by purplish black berries.

It is easiest to buy from a herb nursery a small bay plant which will already be one or two years old. Container-grown plants can be planted out at any time of the year but it is best to plant out all evergreens in showery weather between March and May.

BELOW: Bay, although slow-growing, is a handsome plant

Plant bay in a sunny sheltered position preferably facing south. Do not disturb the root ball when taking bay out of its pot. Dig a hole large enough to accommodate the roots. Put the plant in the hole and gently fill in with soil, firming it down as you go. Tread round the plant to make sure it will not shift in the wind. During the first winter, protect the bay tree by surrounding it with wire netting. Bay can easily be grown in a container which can be brought indoors in a severe winter.

Once bay is established, the fully matured leaves can be picked for use. In August or September stem cuttings can be taken from a strong growing plant but these take a long time to root.

Fragrant aromatic bay leaves are used in many recipes and are well known to all cooks. The leaves can be used fresh or dried. It is advisable to pick and dry some leaves during the growing season for winter use, rather than picking them from the bush all the year round.

Use: Bay leaves are used for flavouring beef or pork casseroles and are a must when poaching or boiling ham or fish. Add a crushed bay leaf to stuffings and made-up meat dishes. A bay leaf put into the water when boiling spaghetti or rice gives a good flavour. Use bay leaves when making pickles and chutneys. It is especially good for pickled beetroot. Bay is one of the herbs in a bouquet garni – the bunch of herbs added to soups, stews or stocks while they are cooking. A small piece of bay leaf can be placed in the dish when making a rice pudding.

BERGAMOT**

Monarda didyma hardy perennial

A strong-growing perennial, bergamot grows about 60 cm (2 ft) high with dark green mint-scented leaves and rather untidy-looking flowers in shades of bright soft red, pink, mauve or white. The red bergamot provides a lovely splash of colour in the herb garden. It flowers over a long period and is a well-known bee plant.

Buy in your first bergamot from the herb nursery in whichever colour you like. From then on you can renew your stock by gathering seed. The seed will come true to

RIGHT: Bergamot flowers provide a welcome splash of colour

form. Sow seed in early spring where plants are to flower and pinch out any unwanted seedlings to leave the plants 30-45 cm (12-18 inches) apart.

Plant bergamot in the autumn in a sunny moist spot in the herb garden. The shallow, fibrous roots soon spread and every two to three years the clump should be lifted and divided. Perform this task in spring as plants divided in the autumn may die completely in the winter. When replanting, use only the newer outside roots. Cut leafy stems and remove the leaves for use to keep the plant trim.

After planting, put peat or leaf mould round the plants to keep the roots moist. The plants die down in winter so use a stake to mark their position. In early spring watch for caterpillars and snails which attack the new leaves.

Bergamot is a useful plant for flower arrangements. To obtain bigger and better flowers for display, cut off all the flowerheads in the first season. The following year there will be a lovely show of much larger flowers.

Use: Bergamot leaves and flowers dry well, retaining their minty scent and flavour. The leaves and flowers can be added to pot-pourri mixtures and used to make a sweet-scented tea. A few dried crushed leaves mixed in with Indian tea adds a delicate flavour.

Bergamot tea is refreshing and soothes a sore throat. Fresh leaves and flowers give a pleasant flavour to summer fruit drinks. Make a sugar syrup adding bergamot, both leaves and flowers. If the flowers are red this gives an attractive colour to the syrup which can be added to fresh fruit salads.

Borage

BORAGE*
Borago officinalis hardy annual
A very colourful herb which grows up to 90 cm (3 ft) high, borage is not recommended for the small herb garden. It self seeds freely and unless it is kept in check you will find borage seedlings coming up all over the garden. The thick stems and rough-textured leaves are covered with hairs. Throughout the summer borage is a mass of lovely clear blue star-shaped flowers. It looks its best grown on a bank or in a raised bed where the drooping flowers can be seen from below.

In early April borage seed can be sown outside where it is to flower. This is important as borage does not transplant well. The seed germinates easily and quickly. Choose a position in full sun and poor light soil. Thin out the seedlings to about 25-30 cm (10-12 inches) apart. In a windy spot it is best to stake the plant because the many-branched fleshy stems become top heavy and after a downpour of rain or high winds will be found lying on the ground.

Borage leaves are always used freshly picked but the flowers, gathered just as they have opened, dry beautifully and retain their pure blue colour. Mix them with other dried herbs in pot-pourri mixtures. Before using the flowers make sure you have removed all but the petals and stamens. **Use:** Borage leaves have a pleasant refreshing taste rather like cucumber. Pick only the young tender leaves with a few fresh flowers and add them to green salads. When greens are scarce, cook and eat borage leaves like spinach with a knob of butter and some freshly ground black pepper. Sprinkle finely chopped leaves over cut tomatoes before baking them and add leaves to cream cheese for stuffed cucumbers. Use some leaves to bring out the full flavour in cucumber soup or sauce and especially when making cucumber chutney.

For a cooling summer drink make a herb tea using both leaves and flowers; leave it to cool then strain it. Mix with lemon juice and sugar to taste and serve well chilled. Add a sprig of borage to cider, apple juice or chilled white wine.

Hot borage tea can be taken as a gentle laxative.

Candied borage flowers make a pretty decoration on cakes and ice creams and floating in a fruit salad. Dip the flowers first in beaten egg white, making sure they are completely covered, then into fine sugar. Leave the flowers to dry and harden on a nylon sieve. Candied in this way the flowers are for immediate use only.

CHAMOMILE*

Matricaria chamomilla (German chamomile) hardy annual
Anthemis nobilis (English chamomile) perennial
Both chamomiles are fragrant feathery-leaved herbs with small daisy-like white flowers, but their growing habits are completely different. The evergreen perennial English chamomile is a low-growing creeping herb mostly used as ground cover or to make a sweet-smelling lawn. It is also a useful edging plant. A variety of the English chamomile called 'Treneague' is non-flowering and cannot therefore cross pollinate with the annual chamomile. This avoids any confusion that might arise because German chamomile is the only variety that you can use in the home.

German chamomile is a charming annual growing up to 30 cm (12 inches) high and very easy to cultivate. Because it self-sows freely the first packet of seed is the only one you're likely to buy. The plants will continue to come up year after year. Each one produces many flowers, the only part of the herb which is used.

German chamomile seed can be sown either in the autumn or early spring. Sow seed in its final growing position in a moist sunny spot and thin out the seedlings to 15 cm (6 inches) apart. Sow English chamomile in seed boxes and transfer seedlings, when large enough, to the open ground. Increase the number of plants by layering the runners or else by dividing the roots in the autumn.

Pick the flowers of German chamomile as soon as they open. Because there will be a continuous supply, it will be a lengthy but well worthwhile task to pick them at this stage when the flowers are at the peak of their fragrance. Dry the flowers on nylon netting in an airing cupboard and store them in glass screwtop jars or add them to your pot-pourri mixture.

Use: The sweet-smelling flowers can be used fresh or dried. The dried flowers keep their lovely scent for a long time. Chamomile tea is a fragrant drink which is both pleasant to take and good for the digestion. An infusion of the flowers used as a rinse on blonde hair will help to keep it a good colour, soft and shiny. To clear the skin and as an effective remedy for a congestive cold make up a strong infusion in a bowl and inhale by covering the head and bowl with a towel, and breathing in the warm fràgrance for about five to ten minutes. A strong decoction can be added to the bath water or a small muslin bag full of flowers placed under the running hot water tap, to perfume the water and provide a refreshing bath which is also good for the skin. Use the infusion for a gargle or mouthwash to sweeten the breath and as a remedy for sore gums.

CHERVIL*
Anthriscus cerefolium bi-annual
So simple and rewarding is it to grow, that chervil must be included in every herb garden. With lacy foliage and clusters of little white flowers, it reaches a height of about 30-45 cm (12-18 inches).

Chervil is a seasoning herb with a mild, delicious flavour. Large amounts can be added to most savoury dishes.

Chervil is raised from seed and, as the plants are small, it is important to provide yourself with a good succession of plants. In the early autumn sow some seed in a sunny position in time for the seedlings to get established before the winter. The plants die down in winter but will come up very early in spring, long before many other herbs appear. When they are large enough, thin the seedlings to 20 cm (8 inches) apart.

In early spring, sow chervil seed in partial shade as the hot summer sun is liable to scorch and discolour the leaves. Always sow chervil where the plants are to grow as seedlings do not transplant well. Successive sowings can be made through the summer months. If the flowers on some of the plants are left to go to seed, chervil will self sow quite happily. Alternatively, gather the seed for the autumn sowing and sow them in a different spot in the herb garden.

Chervil leaves dry well and it is useful to have them through the winter to use on their own or in herb mixtures. They combine well with other herbs.
Use: Chervil makes an excellent herb soup which is delicious served hot in winter. In the summer make a slightly thicker soup and serve it chilled with a little chopped mint sprinkled on top. Use chopped chervil leaves in salad dressings and in green or vegetable salads. Add chervil to sauces accompanying fish or chicken. Chervil soufflé is a light tasty dish and chopped leaves go well in other egg dishes.

Chervil does not have an overpowering taste so you can safely experiment with it, adding chopped leaves to your own savoury recipes.

Chervil is widely used in French cooking. It is added to vinaigrette, bearnaise and ravigote sauces and is one of the herbs in *fines herbes* – a mixture of delicately flavoured herbs used in many dishes.

CHIVES*
Allium schoenoprasum
perennial
Attractive little plants with thin tubular leaves, chives grow about 25 cm (10 inches) high. A clump of chives is essential in the herb garden. Their delicate onion flavour enhances savoury dishes.

The neat growing habit of chives makes them good edging plants in the herb bed. If one or two clumps are left to bloom, their bright mauve pompom flowers provide a gay splash of colour.

Since chives are slow to grow from seed it is easier to start by buying a small plant. Thereafter you can gather your own seed for sowing in the usual way. Clumps which get too big can, in early spring, be dug up and carefully divided. Divide the clumps every two or three years and make sure the new plants are well established before picking the leaves. The whole plant dies down in winter so put in a stake to mark their positions if you are likely to forget where they are.

Plant the chives in sun or partial shade in good soil, spacing the plants about 15 cm (6 inches) apart. At intervals during the growing season feed them with a liquid fertilizer, especially when you see the tips of the leaves going brown. Towards the autumn you can dig up a small clump and transfer it to a container to take indoors for the winter. It will continue growing in the warmth and so give you fresh chives to cut all the year round. In spring the exhausted plant can be thrown out.

Chives can very easily be dried in the oven but remember to dry them on their own or their strong smell will permeate other herbs. Leaves for drying can be cut at any time, but do not cut too many from a single clump at once, unless you feed the soil afterwards. The plant will not survive too severe a cutting.
Use: Chives chopped finely are used to flavour soups, sauces and salad dressings. Add chives to soft cheeses and mashed potatoes. Mix them with parsley to make a herb butter to garnish steak or chops. It is a good flavouring for fish and all egg dishes where only a touch of onion flavour is needed. There are countless ways of using chives and you will find there are many recipes of your own to which you can add them.

DILL*

Anethum graveolens annual

A decorative herb, dill looks at its best when a number of plants are clumped together in the herb bed. The delicate feathery leaves give an almost filmy effect to the plants and the greenish yellow flowers add soft colour. The whole plant grows 60-90 cm (2-3 ft) high.

Dill seed is best sown directly into its growing position as seedlings do not transplant well. In the spring, when danger from frost is over, sow the seed thinly in a sheltered sunny spot and cover the seed with a light sprinkling of soil. When the seedlings appear thin the plants to 25 cm (10 inches) apart. Plants need to be protected from the wind but if a sheltered position is impossible to find in your gar-den, stake the individual plants when they reach 45 cm (18 inches) high. Keep the soil round the young plants free of weeds that compete with the herb for nourishment. Fork the soil over lightly to keep it aerated.

Cut off the flowers of some of the plants as they appear so you can pick and use the leaves. Other plants can be left to go to seed. Once the seeds have formed and are starting to ripen the seed heads should be covered to stop the birds eating them. Tie pieces of muslin or fine netting over the seed heads. The light and warmth will continue the ripening process and you will be sure of a full harvest.

Dill leaves take only a short time to dry and are useful to have in the kitchen during the winter. Seeds take much lon-

Chervil is an easy plant to grow and has pretty, delicate foliage

ger to dry. The method for drying seeds is explained on page 27.

Use: Dill leaves have a delicate flavour which combines well with cucumber. You can add fresh or dried leaves to cucumber soup, sauce and chutney. Use the leaves in potato salad, in cream sauces to accompany fish or chicken and sprinkled over grilled lamb chops.

Dill seed, which has a much stronger flavour, is just as useful as the leaf. Add it to apple pie, bread or cooked cabbage and carrots. Use the seed in spiced beetroot or pickled baby cucumbers. Dill seed tea is very calming, is good for the digestion and will also help you to sleep.

the base white and to make it grow bigger, earth up the bottom when it is the size of a hen's egg. After about ten days to a fortnight the swollen root should be ready to dig up.

Fennel is easily grown from seed and thrives in a sunny sheltered position. In February sow seed indoors in gentle heat so that young plants can be set out into the herb garden in late April. Otherwise sow seeds in April directly into their growing position and pinch out unwanted seedlings. Leave some flowers on the plants to go to seed.

Both leaves and seeds are used in the kitchen; the seeds have a stronger fuller flavour than the leaves. Both can easily be dried for winter use.

Use: Fennel leaves and seeds have a very pleasant liquorice-like flavour. Florence fennel can be eaten either grated raw in salads or cooked and garnished with a butter sauce. Use fennel leaves when cooking all kinds of poached or grilled fish. Add chopped leaves to cheese sauce in macaroni cheese; a few freshly picked leaves add an unusual flavour to a green salad.

Use fennel seed in seed cake and herb breads, and in pasta dishes.

Fennel tea, made with leaves or seeds, is good for the digestion and helps you to sleep. Taken daily first thing in the morning its digestive properties are helpful in a slimming programme. A strong decoction of fennel seed added to yogurt makes a good face pack for toning the skin. A pack made of the leaves alone helps to smooth out premature wrinkles.

FENNEL*

Foeniculum vulgare perennial

A tall handsome herb, fennel grows 1.2-1.5 m (4-5 ft) high. The plant is a mist of feathery bright green leaves and has large flat topped clusters of yellow flowers. It is familiar to those who live near the sea where fennel grows wild along the lanes and clifftops not far from the shore.

A variety of fennel known as bronze fennel because of the colour of its leaves is an elegant plant to use in the

Fennel

background of an ornamental herb garden. Its growing habit is the same as common fennel. Another form of the common plant is the annual, Florence fennel, which grows about 30 cm (12 inches) high and produces fat bulbous leaf stems at the base of the plant. The leaves can be used in the same way as other fennels. The thick turnip-like base is dug up before the plant flowers and eaten as a vegetable. To keep

FEVERFEW*

Chrysanthemum parthenium
perennial

Feverfew bears small daisy-like white flowers which grow in profusion throughout the summer months. The yellowy green leaves have a pungent scent which is somewhat like chamomile. Feverfew is a bushy plant growing up to 60 cm (2 ft) high and takes up little space in the herb bed. Another variety of feverfew has bright yellow flowers and there is one with a very pretty double white flowerhead known as 'Silver ball'.

Feverfew is easily raised from seed. In early spring sow the seed out of doors where it is to flower and it will bloom in the first summer. The seed takes about three weeks to germinate but once the seedlings appear they grow very quickly. Feverfew prefers a sunny position in the herb bed but will flourish equally well in some shade. Pinch out unwanted seedlings, leaving the plants 20-25 cm (8-10 inches) apart.

Feverfew self seeds very readily, and by the second year you will find seedlings coming up all round the parent plant. It follows that you will have no problem increasing your stock of plants, but to ensure that they come true to form, you can take cuttings from the base of the plant in the summer. Make sure the cutting has a heel of the main plant.

Its many tiny flowers make feverfew a useful plant for flower arrangements; it lasts well in water. Both leaves and flowers can be dried successfully for winter use but should be dried separately as the flowers take much longer to dry than the leaves.

Use: As its name implies, feverfew is a medicinal herb, and was originally taken to bring down a fever. Fresh or dried flowers and leaves can be used to make an infusion which is a good remedy for headaches and which, taken over a period of time, is believed to be good for migraine. An infusion of the flowers is helpful for rheumatism.

Feverfew

GARLIC*
Allium sativum annual

A very distinctive strongly flavoured herb, garlic has flat
narrow tubular leaves rising
from a bulb and it produces
tiny bulblets at the top of the
single stem. These should be
removed so that all the plant's
energy goes into the bulb
growing in the ground. All the
flavour of garlic is contained in
that bulb, which is made up of
a cluster of bulblets known as
cloves. Each garlic bulb is
made up of about 9-10 cloves
which are held together inside
a silvery skin. Garlic is an ac-
quired taste but for those who
like it, it is well worthwhile
growing a few garlic plants.
They take up little space in the
herb bed and are a better flavour when used fresh.

Early in spring plant the tiny
bulblets or cloves from a mature garlic bulb. Put them in a
sunny spot in good garden
soil, spaced 15 cm (6 inches)
apart. In mild winters plant
garlic in December or January
so that the bulbs will mature
much earlier.

When the tops of the stems
begin to wilt and bend down-
wards the garlic bulbs are
ready to be harvested. Dig or
pull up the entire plant – do
not remove any of the green
tops at this stage. Lay the
whole herb on wire cake trays
and leave to dry in an airy
room. Gradually the skin
covering the bulb becomes
papery and crackles to the
touch. Finally remove the tops
and save for next year's seed.
Leave the bulbs out for a further two or three days then store
them in a cool place.

The strong flavour of garlic
is not to everyone's taste but,

used sparingly, it brings out
the flavours in many dishes.
Use: Garlic is a useful seasoning herb and in small
amounts, finely chopped, it
can be used in many savoury
dishes – especially with meat
and in casseroles, with chick-
en and added to sauces. A little
garlic juice can be added to
salad dressings. Garlic butter
is made by mixing a crushed
garlic clove with butter.
Spread the butter on to slices
of French bread, wrap the
bread in foil and leave in a hot
oven for 10 minutes. This is
delicious eaten with soups,
salads and cold meats.

HYSSOP*
Hyssopus officinalis perennial

Hysop is neat in appearance,
woody-stemmed, and grows
about 60 cm (2 ft) high. The
small narrow leaves are a dark
glossy green with a strong but
pleasant scent. The little flowers grow in spikes at the top of
the stems and are blue, pink or
white depending on the variety. A clump of the three different coloured hyssops looks
very well in the herb garden
and flowers continually from
July to October. Hyssop is well
known as a bee plant.

In mild areas hyssop re-
mains green throughout the
winter. It is useful grown as a
low hedge.

Hyssop grows well in full
sun and a light soil. It can easily be grown from seed sown in
spring out of doors in its
permanent position. Thin the
seedlings to about 25 cm (10
inches) apart. If only one plant
is required it is best to buy it
from a herb nursery.

with a piece of glass and a sheet of newspaper to encourage germination. As soon as the seedlings appear remove the glass and paper. In July the seedlings can be planted out in their permanent positions. If you want a single plant, buy it from a herb nursery or garden centre. In spring you can increase stock by lifting and dividing the plants.

Both leaves and flowers can be dried successfully. The flowers should be dried separately and can be added to a pot-pourri mixture. After the leaves are dried store them in screwtop jars for use during the winter or add them to the pot-pourri.

Lady's mantle is a lovely plant for flower arrangements of soft hues, used especially with yellow and white. It is chiefly grown as an ornamental plant.

Use: Nowadays lady's mantle is little used in medicine but is still useful as a cosmetic herb. Together with other herbs it makes an effective skin cleanser either in a facial steam or as a lotion. For the lotion, make a strong infusion of the leaves, and leave to cool. Strain and smooth over the skin with cotton wool pads. This is a good cleanser for oily skins. For spots or acne, extract juice from the leaves. Wash them gently, then place them in a clean muslin cloth and twist the ends in alternate directions. Dab on to spots.

Lady's mantle tea is a remedy for diarrhoea and is also helpful to women with menstrual troubles.

You can increase the number of plants by taking stem cuttings in the summer; they soon take root. Hyssop also reseeds itself and the seedlings come true to form. After three or four years the plants become too woody and need replacing. Cut hyssop back after the flowers have died to keep the plant from growing untidily.

A good herb to grow in containers, hyssop can also be grown indoors. Its aromatic leaves have a pleasant scent and it will stay green throughout the winter.

Use: Hyssop is a useful plant for flower arrangements and lasts well in water. Both the flowers and leaves dry well. Remove the tiny flowers from the stems and dry them separately. Add the flowers and leaves to pot-pourri mixtures where they blend well with other dried herbs.

LADY'S MANTLE*
Alchemilla vulgaris perennial
A very attractive herb, lady's mantle can grow up to 45 cm (18 inches) high. Its flat rounded leaves are pale yellowy green and the clusters of tiny flowers, which bloom throughout the summer, are almost the same colour. The plant is a good foil for other herbs in the garden. In some areas lady's mantle will stay green all winter.

Lady's mantle thrives in an open sunny position as long as it is not too dry, and can be easily raised from seed. Sow seed in spring in a garden frame or seed box filled with compost and cover the box

LAVENDER**
Lavendula spica perennial

Such a fragrant plant as lavender deserves a place in every herb garden. An evergreen woody-stemmed herb, it grows up to 60-90 cm (2-3 ft) high. The spiky narrow leaves are greyish green. The flowers are beautifully scented and vary in colour from a brilliant blue to pale mauve, pink and white. All parts of the plant are scented. There is a dwarf form of lavender with the Latin name *Lavendula stoechas* which is a good choice to grow in a container or as a low hedge plant.

Lavender thrives in a sunny sheltered spot in well-drained soil. Buy your plants from a herb nursery or garden centre, because lavender is slow to grow from seed. Evergreens are planted early in spring to give them a full growing season in which to become established. Plant lavender in ordinary garden soil without adding any compost at planting time, and firm the plant down well. To increase the number of plants, take stem cuttings in August from plants which are one or two years old.

Harvest lavender for drying when the flowers are almost fully opened. Cut long stems, tie them loosely together and hang them upside down to dry in the airing cupboard. Place a piece of paper underneath to catch any stray flowers. When fully dried, rub the flowers gently off the stems and store in a screwtop jar.

Use: Add lavender to a potpourri mixture or place a bowl on its own to scent the whole room. Small cotton bags filled with lavender give a lovely fragrance when laid between handkerchiefs or among the linen. Lavender is a good moth deterrent. Added to the bath water it is most refreshing. Tie the dried flowers in a piece of muslin and hang it beneath the running hot tap.

An infusion of lavender flowers dabbed on to the forehead and temples is cooling in hot weather and soothes headaches. You can also use lavender water as an effective skin tonic for a tired dull-looking skin to bring back the colour to your cheeks; be careful not to get it near the eyes. The fragrance clings to the skin for a long time.

Lavender

LEMON BALM*

Melissa officinalis perennial
A hardy plant, lemon balm is a lovely bushy herb for the herb garden with fragrant lemon-scented leaves. Small rather insignificant flowers of white or yellow appear here and there along the stems throughout the summer. The whole plant can grow as high as 90 cm (3 ft) and, unless cut back occasionally will spread over a large patch of ground. Lemon balm dies down during the winter but in some areas after the autumn cutting, new shoots will appear to give leaves through the winter months.

Lemon balm can be raised from seed sown in autumn to make sure of getting good strong plants the following year. The seed takes a long time to germinate so to avoid disappointment buy your first plant from a herb nursery or garden centre. In October or March plant lemon balm in a warm sunny position where the herb will soon become established. Increase the number of plants by taking stem cuttings in the summer or, in the autumn, lift the plant and gently divide the roots. Set out the plants about 25-30 cm (10-12 inches) apart. Lemon balm is a vigorous growing herb and will soon recover after being disturbed.

In the autumn cut back the stems for freezing or drying. The dried leaves retain their lemony scent throughout the winter.
Use: A versatile herb, lemon balm is mainly used in cooking, but it is also a cosmetic and medicinal herb. The chopped leaves, fresh or dried, can be

Lemon Balm

used in recipes wherever a hint of lemon is called for; in chicken or egg dishes, in stews, soups or sauces, added to salads and salad dressings and mixed into cooling summer drinks, especially apple juice. 'Melissa' tea made with the crushed leaves is a refreshing drink sweetened with a little honey and taken hot or cold. It helps to settle the digestion and is a soothing drink taken last thing at night.

An infusion of lemon balm leaves soothes skin irritations and helps to smooth wrinkles. Made up as a herb vinegar, lemon balm dabbed on to the forehead is good for a headache, and the juice from the leaves is a remedy for insect bites and spots.

Add dried lemon balm leaves to a pot-pourri mixture to give it the scent of lemons.

LOVAGE* *Levisticum officinalis* perennial

A large handsome herb, lovage is a good background plant for the garden. A clump of strong thick stems grows up to 1.8 m (6 ft) high. The deep green leaves are much divided and the yellow flowers grow in flat topped clusters much higher than the foliage. The whole plant looks and smells rather like celery, all on a much bigger scale.

Lovage grows well in a moist soil in either a sunny or shady position. It can be raised from seed sown in September in pots or seed boxes filled with compost. Cover the boxes with wire netting to stop the birds eating the seed, and leave the boxes in a sheltered place. In the spring plant out the seedlings 60 cm (2 ft) apart. In a good year lovage will seed itself and in spring the seedlings appear near the parent plant. When starting a new herb garden, it is easiest to buy a container-grown plant.

During the summer, when leaves are needed for cooking, freezing and drying, keep cutting off the flowerheads as they appear. Towards the end of the season leave one or two flowers to go to seed. These can be planted as soon as they are ripe, or dried and used in cooking. In the late autumn lovage dies right down and the old stems should be cut off at the base of the plant.

Lovage leaves freeze and dry well.

Use: The flavour of lovage strongly resembles celery. It is good for seasoning, but should be used somewhat sparingly at first. Lovage soup is delicious and can be made from fresh or dried leaves. Chopped fresh leaves, young stalks or lovage seeds can be added to meat stews in place of celery. Use lovage leaves with boiled ham, in salads and with haricot beans.

A strong decoction of the leaves added to the bath water acts as a skin deodorant.

MARIGOLD*

Calendula officinalis (Pot marigold) hardy annual

Well-known for its bright orange flowers, marigold has a well-earned place in the herb garden. It is an important cosmetic herb and for remedies for minor ailments; marigold can also be used in the kitchen.

It is essential when buying seed that you ask for pot marigold – make a note of the Latin name as there are many different species.

Marigold is grown in the herb garden for its petals so you will need a good number of plants to provide you with sufficient flowers. Use them for edging plants; they grow up to 30 cm (12 inches) high and provide a wonderful splash of colour.

Marigold grows well in sun or shade. In March or April sow the seed where the plants are to flower. Thin the seedlings to 15 cm (6 inches) apart. Marigold self-seeds readily so you will have no problem in providing yourself with plants year after year. Once the seedlings appear you can move them without risk. Alternatively you can collect your own seed and sow it in the spring in

Marigold

the usual way. Marigold is a good plant to grow in containers or hanging baskets and requires very little attention.

Petals for drying should be gathered when the flowers are fully opened and perfect. They are as vivid when dry as when in full bloom.

Use: Marigold flowers have a strong sweet scent and a delicate flavour. Dried marigold petals can be added to a potpourri mixture or used in cooking in place of saffron, to add a soft colour and flavour to rice dishes. Fresh petals bring colour to green salads and can be added to the mixture when making buns or biscuits. Add a few petals to clear soups.

Marigold is a remarkably efficient remedy for minor

skin problems. An infusion of the petals is a refreshing skin toner and helps to keep the skin free of blemishes if used every day. An ointment made with the petals is an effective remedy for sunburn and can be used for acne and skin inflammations. A cool compress using a strong decoction of fresh or dried petals laid over a bruise or contusion will give immediate relief. Marigold oil, made by soaking the flowers in a good vegetable oil for two to three weeks is healing and soothing – excellent for spots and tired feet.

MARJORAM*

Origanum vulgare (wild marjoram) perennial
Origanum onites (pot marjoram) perennial
Origanum marjorana (sweet knotted marjoram) annual
Origanum marjorana var. 'Daphe ffiske' (new perennial marjoram)

The fragrant perennial or annual marjorams should have a place in every herb garden. There is also a perennial golden marjoram to add colour in the ornamental herb bed all the year round. Wild marjoram with its strong spicy taste has small oval shaped leaves and pale pinky-lilac flowers, and grows up to 75 cm (2 ft 6 inches).

Pot marjoram is a handsome herb with deep pink flowers and grows to about 60 cm (2 ft), spreading at least 60 cm (2 ft) across when fully matured. The flavour is not so pronounced as in other marjorams. The sweetest flavour comes from the annual sweet knotted marjoram which grows to about 20 cm (8 inches) and has greeny white flowers like little knots.

Combining the flavour of the two best marjorams is the new perennial marjoram which is a cross between the wild perennial marjoram and the sweet knotted annual. It grows up to 75 cm (2 ft 6 inches) high. The result is the best flavour with the growing habits of the perennial. It is obtainable at specialist herb nurseries as a container-grown herb. All other marjorams can be raised from seed, though some are rather slow to germinate. In early spring, sow sweet knotted marjoram seed under glass and plant out the seedlings in a sunny position when large enough to handle, spacing them 20-25 cm (8-10 inches) apart.

Perennial marjorams can be sown directly into their flowering position and the seedlings thinned to 25-30 cm (10-12 inches) apart.

To increase stock, take stem cuttings from a mature plant in summer. To keep the flavour concentrated in the leaves cut off the flowerheads.

Sweet knotted or the new perennial marjorams are good plants for growing in containers either outside or indoors where they can be in the sun.

Marjoram leaves can be easily dried and sprigs should be gathered just before the flowers appear. Marjoram has a sweet spicy flavour.

Use: The annual or the new perennial marjorams can be used sparingly in meat dishes and in green, leafy or vegetable salads. Make marjoram vinegar to use in salad dressings. Marjoram adds a good flavour to potatoes, dried beans and other bland vegetables. Wild marjoram has a stronger flavour and should be used with care.

Marjoram tea made with sweet knotted marjoram is a soothing drink and a remedy for nervous headaches. A strong infusion of wild marjoram makes an excellent mouthwash.

Pot marjoram

MINT*

Mentha spicata (spearmint)
perennial
Mentha rotundifolia (Bowles
mint) perennial
Mentha piperita (peppermint)
perennial
Mentha citrata
(Eau-de-Cologne mint)
perennial

There are many different types of mint to choose from, each one with highly aromatic leaves and a distinctive scent. Only a few of the best-known mints are mentioned here but you will discover others when you visit the herb nursery.

Spearmint and Bowles mint provide the best flavours for cooking. Peppermint is a medicinal herb as well as being decorative and useful in the kitchen. Eau-de-Cologne mint, sometimes called bergamot mint, is highly scented and decorative. All are handsome plants in the herb garden.

Spearmint grows up to 30 cm (12 inches) tall with narrow pointed leaves and pale lilac-coloured flowers. Bowles mint has rounded woolly leaves, grows up to 60-75 cm (2-2 ft 6 inches) and is a vigorous plant with an excellent flavour. Peppermint has very dark purplish green leaves and grows up to 40 cm (16 inches) high. All mints have a creeping rootstock. There are two prostrate creeping varieties, pennyroyal (*Mentha pulegium*) and Corsican mint (*M. requienii*), which are lovely as edging plants and stay green right through the winter.

All the mints are easy to grow in any position in the herb garden; their chief requirement is plenty of moisture. Mints are invasive growers and in a small herb bed the plants can be restricted by surrounding them with old roofing slates sunk into the ground to a depth of 15-20 cm (6-8 inches). If the space becomes too crowded pull up some of the runners. Mint can be raised from seed or you can buy your first plants from a herb nursery or garden centre.

In spring, sow mint seed in pots or boxes filled with compost and cover them with a piece of glass and newspaper until the seeds germinate. When the seedlings are large enough, set them out in the herb bed 15 cm (6 inches) apart. Mint takes a lot of goodness out of the soil which should be replaced during the growing season, by applying a liquid fertilizer.

Increasing the stock of plants is no problem: simply cut off some of the runners and replant them. Small pieces of root can be laid in a seed box half filled with compost and more compost firmed on top. Keep it moist and new shoots will appear.

A mint bed should be renewed after three or four years to avoid 'rust' disease.

All the mints dry well, though spearmint loses some of its flavour and is best mixed with Bowles mint; both mints can be frozen successfully. Always dry peppermint on its own as it is very strong.

Use: There are countless ways in which you can use the mints, either fresh, frozen or dried. Spearmint and Bowles mint go well in salads, sauces, meat and poultry dishes and in cool summer drinks. Peppermint is delicious in fruit salads and as a syrup poured over ice cream. Sprinkle chopped leaves on to pea soup.

Make peppermint tea for indigestion and add dried leaves to pot-pourri mixtures.

Bowles mint

46

Dry Eau-de-Cologne mint for pot-pourri mixtures or place in small bags on its own to keep among your clothes and linen.

NASTURTIUM*

Tropaeolum majus hardy annual climber

A strong peppery-flavoured hardy annual, nasturtium adds a blaze of colour to the herb garden. Set at the back of the bed where it can clamber freely over a hedge, wall or fence, it looks very attractive. There is a dwarf variety – *Tropaeolum minus* – which is more compact and grows to about 40 cm (16 inches). This is just as colourful as the climber and better suited to a small bed.

Nasturtium has round flat bright green leaves and colourful trumpet-shaped flowers which range in colour from a red-brown through red, orange and yellow to a creamy white. They bloom from July to October.

Nasturtiums are perennial plants but are usually treated as hardy annuals, fresh seed being sown each year. They grow well in a sunny position in sandy soil. In April sow nasturtium seed where plants are to grow. They grow and bloom quite quickly and often re-seed themselves in the same season. To prolong the flowering period cut off the seed pods as they form.

Nasturtium plants are particularly vulnerable to attack from greenfly; as soon as they appear, spray with soapy water. As a preventive try putting mothballs round the plants when they are small.

Nasturtiums grow well in containers both indoors and outside on the patio or trailing from hanging baskets.

Nasturtium leaves can be dried for winter use; the flowers, if successfully dried, add colour to pot-pourri mixtures. Pick leaves for drying just before the plant flowers, and

Nasturtium

pick flowers once opened.

Nasturtium leaves and flowers have a hot peppery flavour and a high vitamin C content which is at its highest in the leaves just before the plant comes into flower.

Use: Nasturtium has medicinal as well as culinary properties. The fresh chopped leaves eaten in a sandwich are a remedy for a cold, though they are good to eat at any time. Juice extracted from the leaves helps to relieve itching.

Chopped nasturtium leaves and flowers can be added to green or vegetable salads, and at the last minute, stirred into a salad dressing. Add a small amount of chopped leaves to cream cheese for a dip or in sandwiches. Make nasturtium vinegar to keep and use for winter salad dressings. Pickle the seed pods while they are young and green and use them in place of capers.

47

PARSLEY**

Parsley

Petroselinum crispum hardy biennial

A deservedly popular herb, parsley has vivid green curly leaves which are particularly attractive in the herb garden as an edging plant. The variety of parsley which is plain-leaved is less eye-catching but has much more flavour. The curly-leaved parsley is useful as a garnish for many different dishes. The variety known as 'Hamburg' or 'parsnip-rooted' parsley is grown for its edible roots.

Though parsley is a hardy biennial, flowering in the second year of growth, it is usually treated as an annual and new seed is sown every year. Plants will sometimes grow on for two to three years – especially the plain-leaved variety which is much hardier than that with curly leaves. Parsley grows up to 30 cm (12 inches) high. If you start by buying a parsley plant pick a small sturdy one which will more readily transplant than a larger parsley. Parsley very quickly puts down a long tap root which will not survive a move.

To grow parsley from seed, first soak the seed in boiling water to help it to germinate; otherwise this can take weeks. In spring or autumn choose a shady spot for the plants and sow the seed there. Pinch out unwanted seedlings to leave 15 cm (6 inches) between the plants. To ensure a long life for the plants cut off all flowering heads in the second year.

Since this herb dries and freezes well, it makes sense to keep some for winter use. Harvest the leaves early in the second year before the plants flower. If flowers are allowed to form the leaves often begin to taste bitter.

Use: Apart from its traditional use as a garnish, fresh chopped parsley is a good seasoning herb to add to meats, casseroles, soups, vegetables, stuffings, salads and with eggs. Parsley not only makes food look appealing but raises its nutritional value as it is full of vitamins. Parsley is essential in herb mixtures as it combines so well with nearly all other herbs.

Parsley tea is an excellent remedy for piles and is believed to help ease rheumatism. A strong infusion of leaves, if used regularly, can help to fade freckles.

ROSEMARY**

Rosmarinus officinalis evergreen shrub

One of the most fragrant herbs to grow in the garden, rosemary is a lovely evergreen shrub which eventually grows up to 1.2 m (4 ft) high. Beautiful soft blue flowers appear in spring, covering the bush with a mist of colour. The flowering period lasts for 6-8 weeks, after which the plant throws up new shoots of its spiky grey-green leaves.

There are several varieties of rosemary. 'Miss Jessup's Upright' is useful as a hedging plant; *Rosmarinus prostratus* is good for ground cover but is rather tender.

It is a slow process to produce rosemary from seed; it is best to start by buying a plant from a herb nursery or garden centre. In April, set the plant in a dry sunny sheltered spot towards the back of the herb garden. Although it is a slow-growing shrub, once the plant is established you can begin to use the leaves. Late summer is the best time to harvest rosemary for drying. In the autumn, cut back half the year's growth on a mature plant. Young rosemary plants need protection during the winter as frost kills the roots. Put a good layer of straw or leaves around the plant and surround it with wire netting. Alternatively, if the plant is not too big, bring it indoors for the winter months.

To increase the stock of plants take stem cuttings or layer one of the branches growing nearest the ground. Summer is a good time to take stem cuttings, so that they can overwinter in a cold frame or greenhouse. Layering can be done at any time during the growing season.

Rosemary dries very well; it retains its strong scent but takes longer to dry than the soft-stemmed plants. Cut off whole sprigs for drying and strip them of leaves after they have dried.

Use: Dried rosemary can be added to pot-pourri mixtures or made up into little bags on its own to lay among your clothes and act as a moth deterrent.

Rosemary has a strong spicy sweet flavour which combines well in both sweet and savoury dishes. Add rosemary, fresh or dried, to roast lamb and to beef or chicken casserole. Sprinkle it over potatoes when roasting and use it with other vegetables. Use it to flavour fruit salads and cool summer drinks.

Make an infusion of rosemary to add to the bath water or to use as a rinse for dark hair. Drink rosemary tea for indigestion; rosemary steeped in oil is a helpful remedy for rheumatism when gently rubbed into the affected part.

Rosemary

SAGE*

Salvia officinalis evergreen shrub

A strongly aromatic herb, sage is a useful plant in the herb garden. There are a number of different sages; the best one for cooking is the narrow leaved garden variety. The flavour is strong but with no hint of bitterness. Sage grows up to 60 cm (2 ft) high, and a mature plant can spread up to 60-90 cm (2-3 ft) in diameter. The coarse grey-green leaves curl inwards when young. Brilliant violet flowers grow out of the bush on tall spikes. Other varieties worth knowing about are: broad leaved sage, which resembles the narrow leaved herb in size and habit but does not flower; purple or red sage, which is mainly ornamental, though the coloured leaves can be used in cooking; golden sage, with a golden variegated leaf, and 'Tricolour' sage which has variegated leaves of white, green and purple-red and is also ornamental.

All the sages can be bought as container-grown plants and planted in spring or autumn in a dry sunny position. In the first year, cut off the tips of the shoots to encourage good bushy growth.

Sage is very easy to raise from seed. In spring or autumn, sow seed in pots or seed boxes filled with compost or out of doors in a seed bed. Transplant the seedlings when they are large enough to their permanent positions. To increase the stock of plants, take stem cuttings in August or layer one or two of the low-growing branches. When layering a branch make sure you cover the cut in the ground with at least 1 cm (½ inch) of soil. Stem cuttings or layering of side shoots are the only ways to increase the number of purple sage plants because its seed does not grow true to form but reverts to the green-leaved sages. Because sage plants become very woody over the seasons they should be renewed every three or four years.

The narrow and broad leaved sages freeze or dry well and retain their full flavour.

Use: Fresh or dried leaves of garden sage should be used sparingly in stuffings, with lamb, pork, poultry and in sausages. Sage adds a pleasant flavour when cooking onions and dried beans. Try adding a few chopped fresh sage leaves to apple juice and cool summer drinks.

Sage tea is a warming drink in the winter and is good for colds and 'flu. An infusion of sage is a good rinse for dark hair, making it shine.

SALAD BURNET**

Sanguisorba minor perennial

A dainty herb, salad burnet is a bushy plant with thin lacy leaves. The small round red flowerheads grow out of a rosette of leaves to a height of 30-40 cm (12-16 inches). The leaves often stay green through the winter months. It has a refreshing cucumber flavour and is both a cosmetic and culinary herb. Salad burnet takes up little space, provides an abundance of leaves for use and is good value in your herb garden. You can buy the first plant from a herb nursery or grow salad burnet from seed. Set your plant in a sunny spot and renew the herb every year, as the full flavour is in the tender young leaves.

In February or March, sow salad burnet seed in boxes filled with a mixture of sand and compost. When the seedlings are large enough, prick them out into pots or seed boxes. Gradually harden off the plants and in late spring set them in their flowering positions 30 cm (12 inches) apart. Salad burnet self-sows freely. To ensure that all the value of the herb goes into the leaves, cut off the flowering heads as they appear.

Salad burnet will grow well in pots or other containers; put them out of doors in summer and bring them in for winter.

Since the leaves continue to appear throughout the winter it is not always necessary to freeze or dry the leaves, but they both dry and freeze well and retain their full flavour.

Use: Salad burnet is principally used as a salad herb providing a cucumber flavour when fresh cucumbers are not available. Salad burnet vinegar is a good base for salad dressings. Use chopped leaves in mayonnaise and with other herbs in a sauce for fish. It adds a refreshing flavour to cool summer drinks. Salad burnet tea drunk hot or cold is a tonic to the system.

An infusion of salad burnet is excellent for the skin when added to the bath water. A strong infusion, used cold, tones and refines the skin. It is refreshing and cooling.

Mixed sages with bronze-leaved fennel, bay, rosemary and young fennel

SAVORY**

Satureia hortensis (summer savory) annual
Satureia montana (winter savory) perennial

Two of the most delightful herbs to grow, summer and winter savory are useful and fragrant plants. Their flavours are similar but their growing habits are different. The annual summer savory grows up to 40 cm (16 inches) high with roundish aromatic leaves and tiny pinky-white flowers. It is a bushy robust little plant, sweet-smelling and quite hardy. Its sturdier relative winter savory is a hardy perennial and grows up to 30 cm (12 inches). The leaves are narrow and lighter in colour than summer savory and the flowers are white. Winter savory grows slowly but neatly into a little mound and in some areas is green through the winter. Both savories make good container plants.

In April or May sow summer savory seed in a sunny position in the herb bed where it is to flower. When the seedlings are large enough, pinch out those not required to leave about 15 cm (6 inches) between the plants.

Buy your winter savory plant from a herb nursery, because the seed is slow to germinate. In autumn or spring plant out winter savory in a sunny spot in light sandy soil. To increase plants, take stem cuttings in August or layer the low-growing shoots. In autumn plants can be lifted and divided.

Summer savory can be grown in pots indoors on a sunny windowsill. Winter savory can be brought indoors for the winter months.

For an annual, summer savory has a surprisingly strong peppery flavour. The flavour

Summer savory

of winter savory is not so strong but is nevertheless delicious.

Use: Both savories are best used when fresh but summer savory dries well and the plant should be harvested for drying when it is in full flower. Often called the 'bean' herb summer savory is particularly good with broad or runner beans. The savories add a good flavour to stuffings for poultry and in meat dishes. Sprinkle a little chopped savory into scrambled eggs. Use winter savory in herb mixtures when making soups and stews.

SWEET CICELY*

Myrrhis odorata perennial

The soft, downy, fern-like leaves of sweet cicely are among the first to appear in the garden in spring. It grows about 60-75 cm (2-2 ft 6 inches) high, but a fully matured plant will spread up to 90 cm (3 ft) in diameter. The flowers form clusters of tiny creamy white blossoms which quickly go to seed. The seeds are large and black when fully ripe. Sweet cicely self-seeds very readily if the flowerheads are not cut off, so once you have purchased your first plant you will have no problem in increasing the number. It is easier to begin with a container-grown plant as seed bought in a packet can be slow to germinate if it is not absolutely fresh. In the autumn seed can be sown for seedlings to appear in the following spring.

In October or March plant sweet cicely in an open sunny position; it also grows quite well in a shady bed – indeed in a very hot dry summer the

leaves are in danger of being scorched. Because the roots of sweet cicely grow very large it is not suitable for container growing. For the same reason, the mature herb, once over a year old, can never be successfully moved to another part of the garden.

In the autumn cut the large stems off at the base of the plant and leave the herb to die right down.

Sweet cicely has a pleasant, sweet, anise flavour and both leaves and seeds dry well. Gather the leaves throughout the summer months and collect the seeds as they ripen.

Use: Sweet cicely is the ideal herb to add to tart fruits like rhubarb and gooseberries; it reduces the acidity, softens the flavours and makes it possible to use less sugar. Add leaves to fresh fruit salads, plums and summer drinks. Sweet cicely is a mild herb and can be used fairly generously mixed with other herbs in salads and salad dressings and when making herb butter. It adds a delicious flavour when cooked with vegetables, particularly cabbage, parsnip and swedes.

An infusion of sweet cicely taken after meals is good for the digestion.

TARRAGON**

Artemisia dracunculus (French tarragon) perennial

A graceful looking plant with narrow pointed leaves and many branching stems, French tarragon is highly aromatic. It grows up to 60 cm (2 ft) high and dies right down during the winter; the tiny greenish white flowers rarely appear and are not known to

Sweet cicely

set seed in this country.

When buying a tarragon plant make certain you get French rather than Russian tarragon. French tarragon has a far better flavour than the Russian which, though it grows into a vigorous spreading plant, seems to lose its flavour as it grows.

In October or March plant tarragon in dry sandy soil in a

sunny position. Good drainage is important, because tarragon will not survive the winter on wet or heavy soils. Once the plant is established, leaves can be picked for use in the kitchen. In September, cut the plant down and freeze or dry the leaves for use during the

winter. In winter protect the herb by covering it with some straw and securing it in place with a piece of wire netting. Remove this in the spring when danger from frost is over. Tarragon will flourish in the same position for some years but, every three or four years, it should be transplanted to another spot in the herb bed to keep it growing vigorously and to prevent any risk of disease. When lifting the plant you can increase your stock by carefully dividing the roots by hand. Set the new plants 20 cm (8 inches) apart. If you lift the plant in October try setting small pieces of root into a pot full of compost and bringing it indoors for the winter. Cuttings of side shoots can be taken in July and placed under a cloche for planting out in the spring. The cuttings may take some weeks to root.

Tarragon leaves freeze or dry quite well but the fresh herb has a superior flavour.

Tarragon

Use: Tarragon is a savoury herb with a strong but delicious flavour. It should be used sparingly in mixtures with other herbs so that they blend well together. Tarragon is an essential ingredient of Béarnaise sauce, and is good in a sauce for fish and a cream dressing for salads. Add chopped tarragon leaves to a leafy green salad and sprinkle them over grilled chops and steak.

Make tarragon vinegar to use in sauces and salad dressing, pickles and chutneys.

THYME**

Thymus vulgaris (common thyme) perennial
Thymus citriodorus (lemon thyme) perennial
Thymus 'Herba barona' (caraway thyme) perennial
There are a large number of different thymes that can be grown for their scent and as decorative plants, but for cooking the best flavours come from the common or garden thyme and the lemon thyme. There is an English wild thyme, still fragrant but with a less pronounced flavour. Caraway-scented thyme or *'Herba barona'*, as it is usually called, is mainly grown as an ornamental plant. Caraway thyme is of matlike growth and is a good ground-cover herb or to use for a path. It bears a mass of lovely, tiny, deep pink flowers and the whole plant has a beautiful scent which is released when the herb is crushed and walked on. There is another ornamental thyme with golden leaves which makes an extremely attractive edging plant.

Common thyme is a small shrubby fragrant perennial growing 15-20 cm (6-8 inches) high with small rounded leaves and pale lilac flowers. Over the seasons it can spread up to 45 cm (18 inches) in diameter. Lemon thyme sometimes grows up to 40 cm (16 inches) high; its leaves, rather darker than common thyme, have a delicate lemon flavour and scent.

All the thymes grow best in a warm dry sunny spot; they can be purchased as container grown plants from the herb nursery, or can be raised from seed. In April sow seed in their flowering positions and pinch out the seedlings to 10 cm (4 inches) apart. Common thyme grows easily from seed; the other thymes are best bought as plants.

The thymes tend to self-layering; to increase your stock of plants in March or April cut off the rooted stems, set them into pots or into the garden and when growing well plant them into their final positions. Every three or four years replant thyme to ensure continued vigorous growth. If the centre of a thyme plant starts to look dead, cover it with soil or compost to encourage new growth.

Harvest thyme for drying when it is in full flower.

Use: Thyme is an evergreen perennial but all varieties, particularly lemon thyme, dry well and are a useful standby in winter. Thyme has a strong delightful scent that blends well in a pot-pourri mixture. It is used in herb mixtures added to soup, stock and stews. Use a little fresh chopped or dried thyme in stuffings and cheese sauces, with potatoes, carrots and beetroot. Add a little lemon thyme to fresh fruit salads.

A tea made from common or lemon thyme is a fragrant drink good for indigestion or a persistent cough. It is also good for insomnia, added to other herbs for a sleep pillow.

VERBASCUM*

Verbascum thapsus (great mullein) biennial

A tall strikingly handsome biennial, verbascum grows to a height of 1.8 m (6 ft). The large grey-green woolly leaves grow in a flat rosette out of which rises a single flowering stem. The stem carries a mass of small golden-yellow flowers early in the second year of growth and flowers over a long period. Verbascum needs too much space to be useful in a small garden, but in a large herb garden it is well worth growing this attractive and useful medicinal herb.

Verbascum grows well in a sunny spot as a background plant. In April sow seed out of doors where the seedlings will get plenty of sun. When they are large enough, thin or transplant the seedlings to 15 cm (6 inches) apart. In April the following year set out the verbascum plants where they are to flower. Leave a few flowers on the herb at the end of the season, for the plant seeds itself very readily. After the second year you can remove the old plants and transplant their seedlings so you will have a constant succession of plants.

Verbascum flowers are the only part of the herb which is used. They can be used fresh or dried for, if carefully dried, they will retain their bright yellow colour. Pick flowers for drying when fully opened and absolutely dry; discard any that are not quite perfect.

Use: An infusion of verbascum flowers provides an effective remedy for chest complaints and in particular a persistent cough. The infusion should be a strong yellow colour by the time you drink it. Once the infusion is made carefully strain the liquid through a piece of fine muslin or cotton to ensure that none of the flowers goes into the drink. For a chesty cold or cough take several cups a day.

Thyme

UNUSUAL HERBS

ANISE*Pimpinella anisum
hardy annual
A mildly scented herb, anise is best known for its spicy seeds. It has feathery leaves and clusters of tiny white rather insignificant flowers. The plant grows rather slowly, to a mature height of about 60 cm (2 ft).

Anise is raised from seed which should be absolutely fresh. Germination is likely to be disappointing if old seed is used. In spring, as soon as the ground warms up and the danger of frost is over, sow anise seed where it is to grow, in light well-drained soil and a sunny position. Thin the seedlings to 15-20 cm (6-8 inches) apart. If you cannot sow the seeds directly into their flowering position, sow the seed in pots or boxes and transplant the seedlings when young and before the tap root gets to any size. Once established it is not possible to transplant anise with success. It is also because of its long tap root that anise is not a good plant for container growing. While anise is growing it is important to keep the soil round the plant free of weeds.

All parts of the plant have a pleasant flavour rather like liquorice. The leaves can be used fresh in the kitchen, but anise is principally grown for its seeds so all the flowerheads are left on the plant to go to seed. In mid to late summer gather the heads when the seeds are fully ripe. Choose a dry day to harvest the seeds and take them indoors to complete the drying process.

Use: The flavour of the fresh leaves is rather strong so use them sparingly at first. Add chopped leaves to curries of meat or poultry, or try a pinch in a savoury pizza topping.

The seeds have a pungent sweet flavour and are delicious used in cakes, bread and pastries as well as in soups and stews. Anise biscuits make an unusual accompaniment to ice cream.

Medicinally, anise seed tea is good for indigestion and for hiccups. It will also help to loosen a dry cough.

APOTHECARY'S ROSE**
Rosa gallica officinalis perennial
One of the earliest roses to have been grown in Europe, the apothecary's rose was so called because the dried petals were widely used in medicines and sold by the apothecary, a chemist who prescribed medicines as well as making them up.

This lovely old-fashioned rose is a beautiful sweet smelling plant for the ornamental herb garden. It is a shrubby perennial growing slowly to reach a height of 60 cm-1.2 m (2-4 ft) when fully matured. The flowers are a deep pink, sometimes mottled, with a delightful perfume and bloom throughout July and August.

The apothecary's rose thrives in a sunny position in any type of soil, and is an extremely hardy plant. Do not, however, take advantage of its accommodating nature by putting a new rose where a rose has been growing before.

Between November and March buy your rose from a specialist or garden centre and plant out in the herb garden when the weather is suitable. Do not plant when there is frost or snow on the ground. The apothecary's rose needs little or no attention but in the autumn any very long shoots should be cut back to keep the plant a neat shape and to prevent too much buffeting by the wind. Apothecary's rose will do well in a wooden tub on the patio or terrace.

Rose petals retain their lovely scent very well when dried. Gather petals for drying when the flowers have fully opened and take only the perfect ones. Dry them in the usual way between sheets of newspaper in a dark airy room.

Dried petals of the apothecary's rose keep their perfume for a long time; enjoy their fragrance either on their own or in pot-pourri mixtures.
Use: You can make your own rosewater using fresh or dried petals. Pour boiling water on to the petals, cover them and leave the mixture to infuse until quite cold. Rose petal water is a refreshing skin toner.

Use candied rose petals to decorate cakes and puddings. Dip dry, perfect petals into beaten egg white and then into sieved icing sugar or caster sugar. Leave them to dry and harden. Jams and jellies made with rose petals have a delicious flavour and rose petal tea, taken hot, is a remedy for chest complaints.

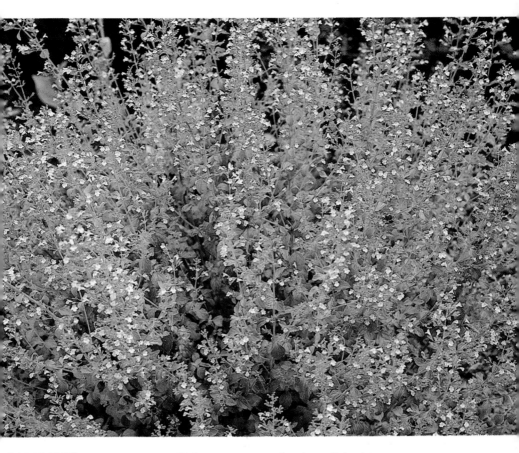

CALAMINT*

Calamintha ascendens perennial
A sweet-smelling, hairy-leaved perennial, calamint is a neat plant that makes a good edging for the herb garden. It grows about 25-30 cm (10-12 inches) tall with small bright mauve flowers which bloom from July to September. The flowers are pretty and colourful but calamint's chief claim to popularity is the lovely minty scent of its leaves.

Buy your first plant from a herb nursery or garden centre, and in the autumn or spring plant it in an open sunny position in the herb bed.

To increase your stock, take stem cuttings in the summer and place them in sharp sand in shallow pots or boxes either in a cold frame or outside and under a cloche. The following spring set them out in the herb garden spacing the plants 15 cm (6 inches) apart. Once the calamint is established it will need a sprinkling of lime round the plant once or twice in the growing season to encourage sturdy growth.
Use: Calamint leaves can be dried for adding to pot-pourri mixtures. Calamint syrup is a useful home remedy for coughs and colds.

Calamint

CAMPHOR*

Balsamita vulgaris perennial
A decorative addition to the ornamental garden, the camphor plant grows up to 75-90 cm (2ft 6 inches-3 ft) high. Its leaves are soft grey-green, its stems stout and square; tiny white daisy-like flowers bloom in great profusion from July to October. Though the whole plant smells strongly of camphor it is not related to the camphor tree which is grown on a large scale in China to produce camphor on a commercial scale.

Buy a camphor plant from a herb nursery in March or October and plant it out in a warm spot in the herb garden.

In summer you can easily increase your stock of plants by pulling off rooted pieces at the base of the plant and setting them elsewhere in the garden, or into pots, to be transplanted later.

The camphor plant grows too large for indoor cultivation, but can be grown successfully in a tub outside.

Once the flowers have opened cut off the plant's long stems. Tie them together loosely and hang the bunches of flowers upside down in a dark dry cupboard until dry and crackly.

Camphor

Use: Strip the leaves off some of the stems and put them into small bags for placing among clothes as an effective moth deterrent.

The camphor plant is excellent for both fresh and dried flower arrangements; it retains its scent when dried.

CARAWAY*

Carum carvi biennial

A hardy biennial, caraway has a bushy growth of feathery leaves and, in the second year, produces clusters of greenish white flowers. The mature plant reaches a height of 60 cm (2 ft) and takes up little room in the herb garden. Caraway is grown for the warm and spicy flavour of its fresh ripe seed.

Caraway thrives in a sunny position in dry light soil. Raise caraway plants from seed sown in autumn or spring where they are to grow. Thin the seedlings to 25 cm (10 inches) apart. If sown in the autumn, caraway plants will be sturdier and produce a crop of seeds the following summer. Thereafter if some seed is left to fall on the ground you will have a continuous crop of caraway each year.

Once the seed heads have formed keep a close watch to see when the seeds are ripe. To make sure no seeds are lost cover the seed heads with fine muslin secured lightly round the stem. This protects the seeds from birds while allowing sunshine and light to finish off the ripening of the seeds. When fully ripe, cut off the seed heads with long

stems, tie the stems together and place the heads in a paper bag. Hang the bunches upside down so that when fully dried the seeds will fall into the bag.

Use: Caraway seed can be used in meat dishes, soups, with cauliflower, cabbage and beetroot and added to cakes, breads, biscuits and cheese. It adds a delicious flavour to baked apples and apple pie.

Sugar-coated caraway seed is a tasty way of settling the stomach after a heavy meal. Caraway is often combined with other seeds such as anise and fennel to make a remedy for indigestion.

CORIANDER*

Coriandrum sativum annual

An unusual annual plant to grow in the herb garden, coriander somewhat resembles plain-leaved parsley in appearance. It is a single-stemmed plant with a long tap root and grows to about 30-45 cm (12-18 inches) high. Small pinky white flowers grow in clusters at the top of the stems and bloom in early summer. In hot countries coriander is grown for its leaves as well as its seed; the fresh leaves, with their sharp distinctive flavour, are sold in the shops as Chinese parsley.

Coriander grows well in a fairly sunny position and a light soil. As an annual, coriander seed is normally sown in April to flower the same summer, but seed sown in the autumn rather than in the spring will produce much sturdier plants. Always sow coriander seed where plants are to flower in the herb bed and pinch out unwanted seedlings leaving plants 25 cm

Coriander

(10 inches) apart. Because of their delicate root system coriander plants will not transplant. Coriander is a pretty herb but until the seed ripens the whole plant has a rather unpleasant smell.

As soon as the seed is ripe, and before it has a chance to scatter, tie pieces of muslin loosely round the seed heads. During July or August when the weather is dry remove the seed heads with long stems attached.

Put the seed heads into a large paper bag securing it so that it does not fall off. Tie the stems together and hang them upside down in a warm dry place. As the seed dries it falls into the bag. After some

weeks the seed should be completely dry and can be stored in screwtop jars.

Use: Fresh young leaves can be used in place of parsley, but go cautiously at first as the sharp rather strong flavour is not to everyone's taste. The chopped leaves are mainly added to hot spicy dishes and sauces.

Dried coriander seed is aromatic and has a distinctive but not sharp flavour. Use it in meat stews and pies, with game and in stuffings for poultry. Add ground coriander seed when baking gingerbread, biscuits and with stewed or baked apples.

CUMIN*

Cuminum cyminum annual
A slender growing annual, cumin is not often seen in the herb garden. It is quite small and inconspicuous with finely cut blackish green leaves and clusters of small dainty pink flowers which provide colour in the herb bed early in the season. Each plant produces a single branching stem and grows up to 30 cm (12 inches) high. A group of cumin plants set together in the herb bed look most attractive. Cumin seed has many culinary uses.

Cumin is raised from seed sown under glass in early spring. Use flower pots filled with compost rather than a shallow seed box as cumin seed needs a good depth of soil in which to grow. Once the seed has germinated and the seedlings are 20-25 cm (8-10 inches) high you can start to harden off the plants, setting them outside on a warm day or putting them into a cold frame. Finally, in early summer, plant out the seedlings in a warm sheltered position.

In a good summer cumin plants go to seed after three months. As soon as the seed is fully ripe, cut down the stems. Tie them together, place the seed heads upside down in a paper bag and tie it loosely in place. Hang the bunch upside down in a dry warm cupboard and the seed, when dried, will fall into the paper bag. After a few weeks check that the seed is well and truly dry then store in the usual way.

Use: Cumin seed has a pleasant spicy flavour and can be used whole or freshly ground. Add cumin to leek soup, meat stews, curries, pickles and chutneys. Use it sparingly in the mixture when baking cakes and biscuits.

GERMANDER*

Teucrium chamaedrys (wall germander) perennial
A very attractive old-fashioned herb, germander was once widely cultivated for use as a remedy for gout. Germander grows 15-30 cm (6-12 inches) high and has creeping roots. The dark green leaves are narrow and pointed; the pretty rose-coloured flowers bloom in June and July. Though the whole plant dies down in the winter, wall germander makes an usual edging plant for the herb garden. Clumps of germander in the front of an ornamental bed look striking when in flower. It is a bitter-tasting herb and the leaves when rubbed have a strong pungent smell rather like sage.

You can buy a wall germander plant from a specialist nursery or raise plants from seed. In early spring, sow seed where the plants are to flower in a sunny spot in the herb bed. The seed can take as long as a month to germinate so mark the place where it has been sown. When the seedlings appear, pinch out those not required to leave about 25-30 cm (10-12 inches) between the plants. The roots spread during the growing season and send up new shoots. In spring or summer take stem cuttings to increase the number of plants.

Use: Originally a medicinal plant, wall germander is now grown as an ornamental plant. The flowers are useful in flower arrangements.

GOAT'S RUE*

Galega officinalis perennial
A lovely herb to grace the back of the ornamental garden, goat's rue is a colourful old-fashioned plant. It grows up to 90 cm (3 ft) high with leaves divided into lance-shaped leaflets. All through the summer goat's rue produces long spikes with masses of little dark blue flowers; there is one variety with white flowers and another with pale blue flowers. Goat's rue can easily be raised from seed or you can buy in one plant of each colour

Jacob's ladder

JACOB'S LADDER**
Polemoneum coeruleum hardy perennial

A showy plant for the decorative herb bed, Jacob's ladder grows 75-90 cm (2 ft 6 inches-3 ft) high. The bright green leaves consist of double rows of leaflets like 'ladders' along the midrib. Numerous flowers of a lovely deep blue bloom continuously throughout the summer. Jacob's ladder is sometimes called 'Greek valerian' in gardening catalogues, but other than in the shape of the leaf it bears no resemblance to the true valerians.

Jacob's ladder can be bought at a herb nursery or garden centre as a container-grown plant. Several varieties are commonly available. There is a very handsome one with variegated leaves and white flowers, and two others which only reach 30 cm (12 inches) in height. One has pale pink flowers and the other has flowers of pale blue.

Plant Jacob's ladder in autumn or spring. An open sunny position is best though it will grow very well in the shade. Once the flowers are over, cut off the flowering stems. In spring give the plants a top dressing of compost or leaf mould. Sometimes the plants will seed themselves, naturally increasing your stock of the herb. Alternatively in the autumn you can lift and divide the plant.

Use: The flowering stems of Jacob's ladder are useful in flower arrangements. The flowers also dry well and add colour to pot-pourri mixtures.

from the herb nursery.

In autumn or spring sow seed in an open sunny position in the herb bed where it is to flower and where the soil is not too dry. Once germinated, remove seedlings not required to leave 30 cm (12 inches) between each plant. An autumn sowing will produce much hardier plants. Set out container-grown plants any time from October to March, provided there is no frost.

In the autumn, when the flowers have died down, cut back the flower stems to the base of the plant. Once goat's rue is established in a good position where it has plenty of moisture, it will continue to bloom for a number of years producing a great show of flowers each summer. The plants may need renewing after three or four years.

Goat's rue leaves have no scent until they are bruised when they give off a rather unpleasant smell.

Use: The only use remaining for goat's rue nowadays is as an infusion of the leaves for bathing tired sore feet.

JUNIPER**

Juniperus communis evergreen shrub

Sharply aromatic, juniper is a lovely plant for the ornamental herb garden. Since a number of different forms are available, both small and large gardens can find room for a specimen. A slow-growing juniper with blue-grey foliage and a spread of 30 cm (12 inches), growing 60-75 cm (2-2 ft 6 inches) high is a most striking plant for a small garden. Taking up more space is a juniper with lush green foliage which again grows slowly but when mature has a spread of 3 m (10 ft) and is only for the large garden.

Juniper thrives in an open sunny position in soil where lime is present. Buy a plant from a garden centre and in early spring set it in the herb bed. No pruning is necessary for junipers. If the tips of the branches go brown sprinkle a dusting of lime around the base of the plant.

In late summer take cuttings of newly growing shoots to increase your stock of plants, putting them into a pot or box filled with sand.

Male and female flowers appear on different plants so to gather juniper berries it is necessary to buy two plants. The berries take two years to mature. In the first year the berries are green; in the second they turn blue-black, ready in the autumn for gathering and drying. They should never be used before they are fully ripe. Juniper berries are gathered singly and can be dried either on nylon netting in a dark warm place or between sheets of newspaper. The berries when dried have a coarse grained texture and a warm spicy flavour. They should always be dried before being used in cooking.

Use: Juniper berries are used to give gin its characteristic taste. In the kitchen the spicy flavour of the berries blends well in beef dishes and with game.

MARSHMALLOW**

Althea officinalis perennial

Tall and stately, marshmallow has soft, velvety, grey-green leaves and small rose-coloured flowers. It grows 90 cm-1.2 m (3-4ft) high and has a spread of 60-90 cm (2-3 ft). This makes it a good choice for the back of an ornamental herb bed where it can protect more tender herbs. Years ago marshmallow was widely used for its medicinal properties and was a common plant in the garden.

Marshmallow is raised from seed sown as soon as it is ripe,

Juniper

but it is easier to buy in a plant from a specialist nursery. It will thrive in any position in the herb garden, though if set in a moist spot it grows very large. Once established marshmallow is a hardy plant which dies down in winter.

To increase your stock of plants sow ripe seed in autumn in a cold frame or seed bed and protect the seedlings through the winter. In the spring set the plants out 45-60 cm (18 inches-2 ft) apart where they are to flower. In the following autumn the plant can be lifted and the roots carefully divided.

Use: Years ago marshmallow root was the part of the herb used, dried and ground, in the making of sweets. A decoction of the root was given to those with chest complaints. It was used as a remedy for diarrhoea. Clean and peel the root before using it fresh or for drying. Marshmallow tea made from the flowers and leaves is still a useful remedy for coughs and colds.

ORRIS*

Iris florentina perennial
An attractive bearded iris, orris is a handsome herb for the decorative herb garden. You can also use the root of the plant in pot-pourri mixtures. Growing 45-60 cm (18 inches-2 ft) high, the light green spear-shaped leaves set off well the fragrant creamy-white flowers that bloom in May.

Orris is easy to grow and thrives in a sunny spot in a limed soil. In July, October or March set out orris plants 20-25 cm (8-10 inches) apart, making sure the rhizomes are near the surface of the soil and

Marshmallow

pointing south.

Over the seasons the plant will gradually take up more space as the rhizomes multiply; if you want to use the herb for pot-pourri carefully take up part of the plant. If this is done immediately after flowering you can divide the plant at the same time, replanting those rhizomes not required for drying.

Orris can also be raised from seed. As soon as the seed is

ripe sow it in sandy soil in a cold frame and set out plants in their flowering position the following spring.

Use: To dry the rhizomes, first scrub them well, making sure thay are free of soil, and cut them into smaller pieces for drying in the usual manner. As the orris dries the scent of violet becomes quite strong, and when the process is complete the pieces can be ground to a powder. Orris acts as a fixative for other scents in a pot-pourri mixture as well as adding its own fragrance.

63

PINEAPPLE SAGE**
Salvia rutilans half hardy
perennial

A lovely shrubby plant, pineapple sage grows up to 90 cm (3 ft) high. It is a tender perennial but well worth growing in the herb garden. The leaves are a deep reddish green and have the sweet smell of fresh pineapple when bruised – the finest scent of all the sages. The flowers, which do not bloom until late autumn, are long drooping spikes of rich red and make a brilliant splash of colour. Unfortunately as the flowers appear so late in the season, in our climate they are caught by frost before they bloom, unless the whole plant is removed indoors for the winter.

During the winter pineapple sage dies down; if it has to be left out of doors it must be protected by covering it with straw held in place with a piece of wire netting pegged down over the top.

Buy your first pineapple sage container-grown from a herb nursery or garden centre. Pineapple sage thrives in a limed sandy soil in a sunny sheltered position. Plant out the herb in spring when all danger from frost is over. In the autumn, either protect the plant for the winter or bring it indoors in a container.

In summer you can increase your stock of pineapple sage plants by taking stem cuttings.

Pineapple sage has no scent whatsoever when dried.

Use: Fresh pineapple sage leaves can be added to fruit salads and mixed into drinks.

ROSE GERANIUM**
Pelargonium graveolens
perennial

The rose-scented geranium is

Pineapple sage

one of the most fragrant of all the sweet-smelling pelargoniums. The dark green leaves are heart shaped and slightly hairy. The flowers, which grow in clusters of five to ten are rather small, purplish-white in colour with dark veins, and the whole plant will grow to approximately 60 cm (2 ft) tall.

Rose geranium is usually grown in containers but can be planted in a warm sunny position in the herb bed for the summer months when danger from frost is over. Before the cold nights of autumn the plant should be brought indoors, potted up in the usual way. Rose geranium is the ideal plant for the small garden or flat dweller because it is a very easy plant to look after and needs very little attention.

Buy your rose geranium from a garden centre and transplant it into a container whether it be wooden trough, tub or flower pot, or keep it in a sunny well drained spot in the herb bed. Geraniums in containers need to be set in good potting compost and once or twice during the growing season should be treated with a liquid fertilizer to keep them healthy and growing strongly.

Rose geraniums can be grown from seed sown in early spring in a pot filled with sandy soil and kept warm. Transfer the seedlings to larger pots when they are big enough. Keep them moist but not too wet.

In August or September, to increase your stock of plants, take stem cuttings, setting them singly in small flower pots of good potting compost. Keep them indoors or in a cold greenhouse until spring – somewhere that is frost free and not too cold. Make sure the cuttings do not dry out completely during this period. In late spring when they are well rooted, transfer the plants to their final containers.

For a winter flowering rose geranium take stem cuttings in early spring and follow the procedure set out above. Stand the flower pots containing the cuttings in a sunny cold frame until September. Transfer the well-rooted cuttings into larger pots and stand the pots where they are to flower on a sunny windowsill.

Rose geranium flowers and leaves can be dried successfully. They retain their lovely rose scent, and can be added to pot-pourri mixtures.

Use: Fresh or dried rose geranium leaves can be used in the kitchen to flavour jams, jellies, cakes, baked custard and ice cream. Rose geranium tea is a refreshing fragrant drink served hot, and is very pleasant served iced on a summer's day.

SOAPWORT*

Saponaria officinalis perennial
Stout-stemmed and colourful, soapwort is an unusual but useful plant for the herb garden. It grows 60-75 cm (2-2 ft 6 inches) high with many very heavily veined leaves. The herb has no scent but is a mass of pale pink flowers from July to September; a number of plants grouped together make a lovely show.

Because soapwort has creeping roots, once it is established plants come up all over the herb bed, so there is no problem when you want to increase your stock of plants. When the plants become too invasive some of them can be pulled up by hand or sliced off with a spade.

Buy a soapwort plant from a herb nursery or garden centre in October and plant it into the herb bed in any position. Soapwort can also be raised from seed. The easiest method is to sow seed out of doors in April in a seed bed, transplanting the seedlings in June or July to their final growing position 15 cm (6 inches) apart. Soapwort needs watering in a dry hot spell. In the autumn the plant dies down and disappears. It is a good idea to mark the spot in case you forget where your soapwort is located.

Use: Soapwort is a cosmetic and household herb. A decoction of soapwort leaves cooled and strained into a screwtop jar is an effective cleanser for all skin types.

A strong decoction of soapwort leaves is a good shampoo. Strain the decoction and scent the shampoo with a little rose or lavender water. The shampoo makes the hair soft and acts as a conditioner.

To make a strong decoction use both leaves and stems. Strain off the herb and use the liquid diluted with warm water for washing delicate fabrics, lace and tapestries.

VALERIAN*

Valeriana officinalis perennial
Handsome and stately, the rich dark green leaves of valerian grow thickly at the base of the herb. One flower stem per plant, which often takes several years to appear, rises 90 cm-1.2 m (3-4 ft) above the foliage and produces clusters of creamy pink flowers. The flowers, which bloom from June to September, have a powerful smell which is most apparent on a hot summer's day. Since early times valerian has been used as a remedy for many complaints and earned itself the country name of All Heal.

Valerian grows well in sun or shade and in a heavy moisture-retentive soil. Plants can be purchased from a herb nursery or raised from seed sown when the seed is fresh from the plant. Sow ripe seed in a cold frame and transplant when the seedlings are large enough to their flowering position. In April sow seed out of doors where they are to grow, pinching out those seedlings not required. Leave

45-60 cm (18 inches-2 ft) between the plants.

Valerian's creeping roots make it easy to increase your stock of plants. In spring or autumn, lift the plant and carefully divide the roots. Set them into their new flowering position and water the plants well until established. If you lift the plant before it flowers the roots, which are the part of the herb used medicinally, are of a much better quality than the roots of older plants.

Clean the roots and grate them into large flakes before drying them in the usual way. Because of its strong smell, it is best to dry valerian away from other herbs.

Use: The lovely shape of valerian leaves make it a favourite with flower arrangers.

Valerian is an effective remedy for sleeplessness. A tea

Valerian

made by soaking the dried root flakes in cold water for twelve hours, is taken about an hour before going to bed.

VERBENA***

Lippia citriodora (Lemon verbena) shrub

A tender deciduous shrub, lemon verbena is a graceful and fragrant herb for the larger garden. The sweet-scented leaves are long and narrow and do not appear until late spring. In August, masses of tiny lilac-coloured flowers bloom at the end of the shoots.

Lemon verbena must be grown in a well-drained sheltered position in full sun. In the right position it will achieve a height of up to 1.8 m (6 ft). Lemon verbena plants too large to be transplanted

into a pot, should be protected out of doors in winter from frost by putting straw or peat round the base and surrounding it with wire netting. Lemon verbena is not a hardy shrub and, where possible, should be potted up and taken indoors for the winter months. After putting the plant in a pot cut back some of the longer stalks and only water it occasionally. These stalks can be planted as stem cuttings in sharp sand, to give you more plants for the following season.

Lemon verbena looks very well in a tub or similar container on the terrace or patio. In winter wrap sacks round the container to keep out the frost.

The beautiful scent and graceful growing habit of lemon verbena make it useful for flower arrangements.

Use: The leaves and flowers dry extremely well and add a lovely perfume to a pot-pourri mixture or put into small cotton bags to hang among clothes and bed linen.

Lemon verbena tea made with fresh or dried leaves is a fragrant drink and a remedy for sleeplessness. Fresh young leaves can be added to fruit salads and cooling summer drinks.

WOAD**

Isatis tinctoria biennial

Woad has attractive long narrow blue green leaves which grow in a flat rosette on the ground in the first year of growth. In the second year the flowering stems grow up to 105 cm (3 ft 6 inches) high, branching at the top and producing a mass of small brilliant yellow flowers. From June to September woad is in bloom and the flowers are followed by long blue black seeds. The whole plant is tall, sturdy and conspicuous and is best grown at the back of the bed. Both flowers and seeds make unusual flower arrangements.

Woad was traditionally used for its blue dye which was prepared from the leaves and stems. Nowadays it is grown commercially on a small scale.

A hardy biennial, woad will readily seed itself. Once established in the garden you will have a lovely clump of woad year after year.

Woad thrives in a sunny position in good garden soil. Buy in your first plant from a herb nursery or raise the plants from seed. Woad seed is sown in August where the plants are to flower. Pinch out those seedlings not required to leave the plants about 25 cm (10 inches) apart.

WOODRUFF**

Asperula odorata (sweet woodruff) perennial

A very attractive ground cover plant for shady areas, sweet woodruff has narrow deep green leaves set in rosettes up the stem. The tiny star-shaped flowers are white and sweet-scented, and bloom in May and June. The whole plant is very dainty and does not grow higher than 20-25 cm (8-10 inches). Woodruff will grow quite happily in the shade of a larger plant such as sage or bay tree in the herb garden.

Sweet woodruff can be raised from seed sown in July or August but germination is exceedingly slow and the seed needs to be absolutely fresh. It is easier to buy in your first few plants in the spring from a herb nursery and set them into the herb bed 15-20 cm (6-8 inches) apart. During the early summer, just after flowering, you can increase your stock of plants by lifting and dividing the roots. Thereafter the creeping roots of sweet woodruff will gradually spread over the ground providing a dense high mat. Sweet woodruff leaves have no scent when fresh but smell like new-mown hay when dried.

Use: The leaves of sweet woodruff dry well and can be used in small bags laid among clothes to keep away moths. Dried or wilted sweet woodruff can be added to Rhine wine to make a delightful exhilarating drink. Sweet woodruff tea made with dried leaves is a soothing, calming drink and a remedy for headaches.

Woodruff

HERB GROWING THROUGH THE SEASONS

A = Annual – a plant which grows from seed, comes to maturity and dies within one year
B = Biennial – a plant which vegetates one year and flowers, fruits and dies in the second
P = Perennial – a plant that lives more than two years

HERB	A B P Ba E	SPRING	SUMMER
ANGELICA *Angelica archangelica*	B 1.8m (6 ft)	Plant container-grown herb in partial shade at back of bed. Transplant seedlings growing around parent plant.	Cut off flowerheads as they appear. Leave one or two to set seed. Sow ripe seed in Aug. in seed bed or boxes out of doors.
ANISE *Pimpinella anisum*	A 60 cm (2 ft)	Sow seeds where plants are to flower in sunny position. Thin seedlings 15-20 cm (6-8 in) apart.	Keep soil round plants free of weeds. Gather seed when fully ripe in late summer.
APOTHECARY'S ROSE *Rosa gallica officinalis*	P 60 cm- 1.2 m (2-4 ft)	In March plant rose in sunny position or in a container on terrace.	Pick petals for drying throughout summer.
BASIL *Ocimum basilicum*	Half hardy A 30-60 cm (1-2 ft)	Sow seed in gentle heat. Prick out seedlings into pots. Keep pots in greenhouse or indoors.	Plant seedlings 15-20 cm (6-8 in) apart in sunny sheltered position. Pinch out flowers as they appear until end of season. Leave some to set seed.
BAY *Laurus nobilis*	E tree up to 12 m (40 ft)	Between March and May plant container-grown bay in sunny sheltered position in herb bed, or plant in tub or pot for terrace.	Pick leaves from established plants.
BERGAMOT *Monarda didyma*	P 60 cm (2 ft)	Sow seed where plants are to flower. Thin seedlings to 30-45 cm (12-18 in) apart. Lift and divide mature plants.	Put peat or leaf mould round plants to keep roots moist.
BORAGE *Borago officinalis*	A 90 cm (3 ft)	In April sow seed where plants are to flower in sunny position.	Thin seedlings to 20 cm (10 in) apart. Harvest flowers.
CALAMINT *Calamintha ascendens*	P 25-30 cm (10-12 in)	In March buy plant and set in open sunny position. Plant out last year's cuttings 15 cm (6 in) apart.	Sprinkle lime round base of plant. Take stem cuttings and set them in boxes of sharp sand. Leave in cold frame or outside.
CAMPHOR *Balsamita vulgaris*	P 75 cm (2 ft 6 in)	In March buy container-grown herb. Set in sunny position.	Flowers in bloom. When fully open cut off long stems for drying. Take rooted pieces from base of plant to increase stock.

Ba = Bi-annual – a plant that flowers and fruits twice in one year
E = Evergreen – a plant in leaf throughout the year

AUTUMN	WINTER	USES
Clear away old flowering stems and dead leaves.	Plant dies right down. In 2nd winter, after flowering, plant dies.	Candied young stems as flavouring. Young leaves in poached fish and rhubarb jam. Seeds to flavour custard. Tea for feverish cold.
Once seed is harvested remove old plants.		Seed in soups and stews, cakes, bread and pastries. Seed tea for indigestion and dry cough.
Cut back long shoots to neaten the shape.	Rose may also be planted in November (see 'Spring').	Make rose water from petals fresh or dried. Candied rose petals for cakes and puddings. Rose petal jam. Rose petal tea, remedy for chest complaints.
In late Autumn pull up plants and keep any seed for next year's plants.		Leaves in tomato dishes, with minced beef and sausages. Small amount in butter sauces on peas and boiled potatoes.
Aug-Sept take stem cuttings.	Bay in pots or tubs can be brought indoors for winter.	Leaves in meat casseroles and in stuffings. Add to water when boiling rice or spaghetti. In pickles and chutneys, bouquet garni, rice pudding.
Plant container-grown bergamot in sunny moist position.	Plants die down. Mark site with stake.	Flower arrangements. Dried in pot-pourri. Bergamot syrup in summer fruit salads. Tea for sore throat. Bee plant.
Continue harvesting flowers.	Dig up old plants.	Young leaves and flowers in salads, summer drinks. Leaves with tomatoes, cucumber. Candied flowers as cake decoration.
Cover cuttings with cloche.	Cut back flowering stems.	Edging plant. Dried leaves in pot-pourri. Syrup for coughs.
In October buy container-grown herb and set in sunny position.	Dies right down. Cut back old woody stems.	Fresh or dried in flower arrangements. Dried leaves are moth deterrent.

HERB	A B P Ba E	SPRING	SUMMER
CARAWAY *Carum carvi*	B 60 cm (2 ft)	Sow seed where plants are to grow in a sunny position. Thin seedlings to 25 cm (10 in) apart.	Cover seed heads with muslin.
CHAMOMILE German *Matricaria chamomilla* English *Anthemis nobilis*	A 30 cm (12 in) P	In early spring sow annual seed where it is to flower in sunny position. Sow perennial seed in boxes.	Thin seedlings to 15 cm (6 in) apart. Transplant perennial seedlings to open ground. Pick flowers of annual when open.
CHERVIL *Anthriscus cerefolium*	Ba	Sow seed in partial shade.	Make successive sowings throughout summer. Leave flowers on some plants to set seed and self sow.
CHIVES *Allium schoenoprasum*	P 25 cm (10 in)	Buy herb and plant bulbs 15 cm (6 in) apart in sun or partial shade. Lift and divide established clumps.	Cut off flowerheads. Cut leaves for drying. Feed clumps with liquid fertilizer.
CORIANDER *Coriandrum sativum*	A 30-45 cm (12-18 in)	In April sow seed where plants are to grow. Thin seedlings to 25 cm (10 in) apart.	Tie pieces of muslin over seed heads.
CUMIN *Cuminum cyminum*	A 30 cm (12 in)	In early spring sow seed under glass. Harden off seedlings when 20-25 cm (8-10 in) high.	Set plants in warm sheltered position. When seeds are ripe cut down stems for drying.
DILL *Anethum graveolens*	A 60 cm (2 ft)	Sow seed in sunny sheltered position.	Thin seedlings to 25 cm (10 in) apart. Keep plants weed free. Cut off flowerheads. Leave some to set seed.
FENNEL *Foeniculum vulgare*	P 1.2m (4 ft)	In April sow seed in permanent position in sun at back of herb bed.	Thin seedlings to 30 cm (12 in) apart. Cut off flowers. Earth up bulbous fennel. Harvest as required.
FEVERFEW *Chrysanthemum parthenium*	P 60 cm (2 ft)	In early spring sow seed outdoors in sunny spot. Thin seedlings 20 cm (8 in) apart.	Take cuttings from base of plant.
GARLIC *Allium sativum*	A	Plant bulblets (cloves) from mature herb in sunny position. Space 15 cm (6 in) apart.	
GERMANDER *Teucrium chamaedrys*	P 15-30 cm (6-12 in)	Buy plant and set in sunny position. In early spring sow seed where plants are to grow.	Thin seedlings to 25 cm (10 in) apart. Take stem cuttings.
GOAT'S RUE *Galega officinalis*	P 90 cm (3 ft)	Buy plants and set in sunny position at back of herb bed. Sow seed where it is to flower.	Thin seedlings to 30 cm (12 in) apart.

AUTUMN	WINTER	USES
Sow seed where plants are to grow in a sunny position. Gather seed heads for drying.	Dry seeds.	Seed in soups with meat, cabbage, cauliflower, beetroot. Add to cakes, biscuits, apple pie. Seed tea for indigestion.
Annual seed can be sown in growing position and seedlings thinned to 15 cm (6 in) apart. Layer runners or divide roots of perennial plants.	Remove dead annual plants.	Dried flowers in pot-pourri. Tea for indigestion. Infusion as rinse for blonde hair, to clear the skin, for colds.
Early autumn sow seed in sunny position. Thin seedlings to 20 cm (8 in) apart.	Remove all dead plants.	Dried leaves in herb soup. Fresh or dried leaves in salad dressings, salads, soufflé, sauces.
Pot up a clump to take indoors.	Plants die down. Mark positions.	Fresh or dried leaves in soups, sauces, salads, herb butter, soft cheese, mashed potato, egg and fish dishes.
Remove seed heads for drying. Sow seed where plants are to grow. Thin seedlings to 25 cm (10 in) apart.	Leave seeds to continue drying.	Chopped fresh leaves in hot spiced sauces. Dried seed in meat stews, pies, in stuffings; ground seed in biscuits, ginger bread.
Remove old plants.	Dry seeds.	Dried seed in leek soup, meat stews, curries, pickles, chutneys. Ground seed in cakes and biscuits.
Early autumn tie muslin over seed heads to protect from birds.	Dry seeds.	Fresh or dried leaves in salads, cucumber sauce, cream sauces. Seeds in apple pie, spiced beetroot, with cabbage, carrot.
Leave one or two flowerheads to set seed. Harvest bulbous fennel as required.	In February sow seed in gentle heat.	Eat bulbous fennel as vegetable. Fresh or dried leaves with fish, cheese, in salads. Tea for digestion. Seed for toning skin.
Dry flowers and leaves for winter. Plant self-seeds freely.		Flower arrangements. Infusion of leaves and flowers for headache, migraine. Infusion of flowers for rheumatism.
Dig up whole plant to harvest bulbs when stems wilt.	Remove tops. Leave bulbs to dry a few more days.	Sparingly in savoury dishes, meat, chicken, sauces. Juice in salad dressings. Garlic bread.
	Plant dies down.	Ornamental; edging plant.
Sow seed where plant is to flower. Thin seedlings to 30 cm (12 in) apart.	Cut back flowering stems to base of plant. Plant dies down.	Ornamental. Infusion of leaves for tired feet.

HERB	A B P Ba E	SPRING	SUMMER
HYSSOP *Hyssopus officinalis*	P 60 cm (2 ft)	Sow seed outdoors in sunny position, or buy plant.	Thin seedlings to 25 cm (10 in) apart. Take stem cuttings from established plant.
JACOB'S LADDER *Polemoneum coeruleum*	P 75 cm (2 ft 6 in)	Buy plant and set in sunny or shady position. Top dress established plants with compost.	
JUNIPER *Juniperus communis*	E 75 cm (2 ft 6 in) or 3 m (10 ft)	Buy plant, set in open sunny position. Buy male and female plants for berries.	Take cuttings of new shoots.
LADY'S MANTLE *Alchemilla vulgaris*	P 45 cm (18 in)	Buy plant and set in sunny spot. Sow seed in cold frame. Lift and divide established plants.	In July plant seedlings 25 cm (10 in) apart in sunny position.
LAVENDER *Lavendula spica*	E 60 cm (2 ft)	Buy plants and set in sunny sheltered position. Can be grown as hedge plant or in containers on terrace.	In August take stem cuttings from 2-year-old plants.
LEMON BALM *Melissa officinalis*	P 90 cm (3 ft)	In March buy plant and set in sunny position.	Take stem cuttings.
LOVAGE *Levisticum officinalis*	P 1.8 m (6 ft)	Plant seedlings from autumn sowing in sunny spot 60 cm (2 ft) apart, or buy plant.	Cut off flowerheads as they appear.
MARIGOLD *Calendula officinalis*	A 30 cm (12 in)	Sow seed in permanent position in sun or shade. Thin seedlings 15 cm (6 in) apart. Plant in tubs and containers.	Good edging plant. Self-seeds freely.
MARJORAMS *Origanum* spp.	A/P 20 cm (8 in)	Buy perennial marjoram plants and set in sunny position 25 cm (10 in) apart. Sow annual seed under glass.	Plant out seedlings 20 cm (8 in) apart. Take stem cuttings from mature plants.
MARSHMALLOW *Althea offiicinalis*	P 90 cm (3 ft)	Buy plant and set at back of herb bed. Set out plants 45 cm (18 in) apart where they are to flower.	Keep well watered.

AUTUMN	WINTER	USES
After flowering cut back the plant to one third of year's growth. Reseeds itself.	In mild areas stays green all winter.	Ornamental. Flower arrangements. Dried flowers and leaves in pot-pourri. Bee plant.
Buy plant and set in sunny or shady position. Lift and divide mature plants to increase stock.		Ornamental. Flower arrangements. Dried flowers in pot-pourri. Bee plant.
Sprinkle lime round plant when tips of branches are brown.	Dry berries.	Ornamental. Dried berries in beef dishes, with game.
Cut off flowering stems.	In some areas stays green all winter.	Ornamental. Flower arrangements. Fresh or dried leaves as skin cleanser. Juice for spots and acne. Dried flowers in pot-pourri.
Trim back stems at end of flowering period.	Protect 1-year-old plants with straw and wire netting.	Ornamental. Dried flowers in pot-pourri, in lavender bags. Lavender water as skin tonic. Infusion dabbed on for headaches.
Cut back stems to base of plant. Sow seed outdoors in sunny position. Thin seedlings 25 cm (10 in) apart. Lift and divide roots to increase stock.	Dies down in winter. In mild winter new shoots appear.	Fresh or dried leaves with chicken, in soups, sauces, salads. In cooling drinks. 'Melissa' tea for indigestion. Juice of leaves for bites. Dried leaves in pot-pourri.
In September, sow fresh seed in pots or boxes. Cover with wire netting. Leave outside in sheltered place.	Plant dies down in winter. Remove old flowering stems and dead leaves.	Fresh or dried leaves as herb soup. Add to meat dishes in salads, with haricot beans, baked or boiled ham.
Clear away dead plants.	Keep self-sown seedlings free of weeds.	Dried petals in pot-pourri. Fresh or dried petals in place of saffron. Infusion as skin toner. Ointment for skin complaints, sunburn.
Cut back flowering stems. Pull out annuals.	Divide perennial plants.	Fresh or dried leaves in meat dishes, vegetable salads, stuffings. Add to potatoes, dried bean dishes. Marjoram vinegar in salad dressings. Tea for headaches.
Sow seed in cold frame or seed bed. Lift and divide established plants.	Protect seedlings through winter.	Dried root as flavouring. Decoction of root for chest complaints. Tea of flower and leaves for coughs and colds.

HERB	A B P Ba E	SPRING	SUMMER
MINT *Mentha* spp.	P 30-60 cm (12-24 in)	Buy plants and set in moist shady spot. Sow seed in pots.	Plant seedlings 15 cm (6 in) apart in moist shady position. Water plants with liquid fertilizer.
NASTURTIUM *Tropaeolum majus*	hardy A climber	Sow seed in permanent position in full sun. Good container plants.	Plants reseed themselves.
ORRIS *Iris florentina*	P 45 cm (18 in)	In March buy plants out 20 cm (8 in) apart in sunny position. Set out plants sown in previous autumn.	After flowering lift and divide plants. Keep some rhizomes for drying.
PARSLEY *Petroselinum crispum*	B 30 cm (12 in)	Buy plant. Soak seed in boiling water and sow in shady spot. Thin seedlings to 15 cm (6 in) apart.	Cut off flowers in second year to prolong life of plant.
PINEAPPLE SAGE *Salvia rutilans*	P 90 cm (3 ft)	Buy plant and set in sunny sheltered position. Suitable for pots or tubs.	Take stem cuttings to increase stock.
ROSE GERANIUM *Pelargonium graveolens*	P 60 cm (2 ft)	Buy plant and set into tub or other container. Sow seed in sandy soil in gentle heat.	Set out plant in sunny position. Give pot plants liquid fertilizer.
ROSEMARY *Rosmarinus officinalis*	E 1.2 m (4 ft) shrub	Buy plant in April and set in sunny sheltered spot at back of herb bed.	Layer low-growing branches of mature plants. Take stem cuttings of new shoots – overwinter in cold frame or greenhouse.
SAGE *Salvia officinalis*	E shrub 60 cm (2 ft)	Buy plant and set in dry sunny position. Sow seed in pots. Set out seedlings 45 cm (18 in) apart.	Cut off tips of shoots in 1st year to encourage bushy growth. Take stem cuttings or layer low-growing side shoots of mature plants.
SALAD BURNET *Sanguisorba minor*	P 30 cm (12 in)	Buy plant and set in sunny position. Sow seed in boxes, harden off plants. Good plant for tubs.	Transplant seedlings to permanent position 30 cm (12 in) apart. Self-sows freely if left to flower.
SAVORY Summer savory *Satureia hortensis* Winter savory *Satureia montana*	A 40 cm (16 in) P 30 cm (12 in)	Buy plant, set in sunny position. Annual savory in pot on sunny windowsill.	Sow annual seed in sunny position. Thin seedlings to 15 cm (6 in). Take stem cuttings of perennial plant.

AUTUMN	WINTER	USES
Remove old flowering stems. Remove runners and plant in boxes to increase stock for next year.	Plants die down in winter.	Fresh or dried leaves in sauces, salads, meat, poultry; with fruit, ice cream. Dried leaves in pot-pourri.
Remove old plants.		Full of vitamin C. Fresh leaves in sandwiches, green and vegetable salads. Nasturtium vinegar for salad dressings.
Buy plants and set in sunny position. Sow seed when ripe in cold frame.		Dried rhizome ground in pot-pourri.
Soak seed in boiling water, then sow in permanent position in shady spot. Thin seedlings to 15 cm (6 in) apart.	Plants die down.	Fresh or dried leaves in all savoury dishes. Full of vitamins. Parsley tea for piles. Infusion for freckles.
Where possible bring plants indoors.	Indoor plants flower in November. Protect outdoor plants with straw and wire netting.	Ornamental. Fresh leaves in fruit salads and fruit drinks.
Take stem cuttings. Keep indoors until early summer.	Keep plants in frost-free place.	Dried flowers and leaves in pot-pourri. Fresh or dried leaves in jams, jellies, cakes, custards. Tea as refreshing drink.
Cut back half the year's growth on established plants. Bring small plants indoors if possible.	Protect young plants with straw and wire netting.	Add fresh or dried leaves to meat dishes, vegetables and fruit salads. Infusion as rinse for dark hair. Tea for indigestion. Rosemary oil for rheumatism.
Renew sage plants after about 4 years when very woody. Cut back half the year's growth.		Fresh or dried leaves in meat dishes, poultry, dried beans. Fresh leaves in apple juice. Sage tea for colds and 'flu'. Infusion as rinse for dark hair.
Cut back flowering stems	Plant outdoors. Stays green through winter.	A salad herb. Vinegar in salad dressings. In herb mixtures. With fish, cool summer drinks. Infusion as skin tonic.
Buy plant and set in sunny position. To increase stock lift and divide perennial plants.	In some areas perennial stays green through winter. Pot of perennial can be brought indoors.	The 'bean' herb – add fresh or dried savory to all bean dishes. Use in stuffings and herb mixtures.

HERB	A B P Ba E	SPRING	SUMMER
SOAPWORT *Saponaria* *officinalis*	P 60 cm (2 ft)	In April sow seed in seed bed.	In June transplant seedlings 15 cm (6 in) apart, any position. Water in dry spell.
SWEET CICELY *Myrrhis odorata*	P 60 cm (2 ft)	Buy plant and set in open sunny position. Transplant seedlings from autumn sowing 45 cm (18 in) apart.	Self-seeds freely if left to flower.
TARRAGON *Artemisia* *dracunculus*	P 60 cm (2 ft)	Buy plant in March. Set in dry sunny spot.	Take cuttings of side shoots, keep under cloche for planting out in spring.
THYME *Thymus* spp.	P 20-45 cm (8-18 in)	In March cut off rooted stems of mature plants. Buy plants and set in warm dry sunny spot. Sow common thyme seed in April.	Thin seedlings 10 cm (4 in) apart. Keep weeds down round tiny plants. Harvest for drying when in flower.
VALERIAN *Valeriana* *officinalis*	P 90 cm (3 ft)	Buy herb; plant in sun or shade. In April sow seed in flowering position. Lift and divide mature plants.	Thin seedlings to 45 cm (18 in) apart.
VERBASCUM *Verbascum* *thapsus*	B 1.8 m (6 ft)	Sow seed in April in sunny spot. Thin seedlings 15 cm (6 in) apart. Following April set in permanent position 30 cm (12 in) apart.	Harvest flowers every morning.
VERBENA Lemon verbena *Lippia citriodora*	P shrub 1.8 m (6 ft)	Buy plant and set in sunny sheltered position.	Harvest leaves.
WOAD *Isatis tinctoria*	B 105 cm (3 ft 6 in)	Buy herb and set in sunny position.	In August sow seed in permanent position. Thin seedlings 25 cm (10 in) apart.
WOODRUFF *Asperula odorata*	P 20 cm (8 in)	Buy plants and set 15 cm (6 in) apart in shade of larger herb or shrub.	To increase stock of plants, lift and divide roots. In July or August sow seed, thin to 15 cm (6 in) apart. Harvest flowering stems.

AUTUMN	WINTER	USES
In October buy plant and set in any position.	Plant dies right down. Mark spot with stake.	Decoction of leaves as skin cleanser, shampoo. Decoction of whole plant for washing delicate fabrics.
Cut back flowering stems and dead leaves. Sow fresh seed in boxes. Leave outdoors in sheltered spot.	Plant dies down.	Cuts acidity when added to tart fruits such as rhubarb or gooseberry. Leaves in fruit salads, with plums, in salads and salad dressings.
Buy plant in October, set in dry sunny spot. Lift and divide old plants and set 20 cm (8 in) apart.	Protect plant from frost by covering with straw and wire netting.	Savoury herb. Use in sauces and salads; sprinkle over grilled chops and steak. Tarragon vinegar in salad dressings, pickles, chutneys.
Thymes are self-layering. Trim plant if it becomes straggly.	Cover dead-looking centres of old plants with soil or compost to encourage new growth in spring.	Fresh or dried leaves in soups, stews, stuffings, with cheese and vegetables. Thyme tea for cough. Lemon thyme to fresh fruit salads, in pot-pourri.
Sow ripe seed in cold frame. Lift and divide mature plants. Keep some roots for drying. Transplant seedlings 45 cm (18 in) apart.	Plant dies down.	Flower arrangements. Tea for sleeplessness.
Leave some flowers on plant to self-seed.	At end of 2nd year remove old plants.	Fresh or dried flowers remedy for coughs. Dried flowers in pot-pourri.
Take stem cuttings and overwinter in greenhouse or indoors. Take plant indoors for winter – cut back long stems.	Wrap sack round containers standing on terrace to keep out frost. Protect outdoor plants with straw and wire netting.	Flower arrangements. Dried leaves and flowers in pot-pourri, in bags to hang among clothes. Fresh leaves in fruit salads.
Mark position of plant.		Ornamental. A dye plant.
Cut back dead flowerheads.	Dies down in winter.	Dried leaves among clothes to deter moth. Dried or wilted leaves in Rhine wine. Tea soothes headaches.

INDEX

ACKNOWLEDGMENTS

The following photographs were taken specially for
Octopus Books:
Michael Boys 1, 2, 5, 21, 31, 32, 33, 39, 40-1, 43, 44, 45,
51, 53, 54, 64, 80; Jerry Harpur 38, 66; Neil Holmes 42,
46-7, 49, 52, 55, 57, 58, 59, 62, 63; Octopus Books Ltd 48;
George Wright 13, 47.

The publishers would like to thank the following
organisations and individuals for their kind permission to
reproduce the photographs in this book:
Heather Angel 34, Marie Louise Avery 67; Brian Furner
Photographic Collection 37, 60-1.
All illustrations by Lindsay Blow.